Praise for *Rewilding the Church*

This is an exciting and surprising bringing together of two very different themes, which on reflection most naturally belong to each other. A clear, easy and liberating read.

Revd Dr Michael Moynagh, author of Church for Every Context *(2012) and* Church in Life: Innovation, Mission and Ecclesiology *(2017)*

Steve Aisthorpe challenges us to stop and to pay attention to what is right in front of us. His deep and abiding love for Christ, creation and the Church are evident on every page, drawing profound lessons about church, mission and leadership from an ecosystem greatly damaged by human intervention, and yet with tremendous powers of recovery. It is filled with fascinating information, deep questions about the Church's response to the challenges it faces, and with an undiminished trust in the God of past, present and future. Whether you agree with every point he makes or not, this will get you thinking, it will start conversations, and will provoke change. Everyone involved in mission and leadership should add this to their 'must read' list.

Lesley Hamilton-Messer, Church Without Walls Team Leader, Church of Scotland

Metaphors can be powerful. Well-chosen metaphors can be transformative. Fresh metaphors can take us by surprise and force us to see old problems in a new light. In this book Steve Aisthorpe sets a fresh and startling metaphor to work, forcing us to re-think strategy for the future of the Church.

The metaphor of rewilding the Church is powered by current trends in ecology and environmentalism and by Aisthorpe's astute reading of the sacred scriptures.

Leslie J. Francis, Professor of Religions and Psychology, University of Warwick

In this, his second book, Steve Aisthorpe applies further insights from his conversations with former churchgoers to build an exciting, new model of what God may be up to and what the Church can become. His engaging style encourages both reflection and the use of our imagination, as we ponder how the ecological notion of 'rewilding' might be brought to bear on our response to God's call.

David Walker, Bishop of Manchester

Few books are essential reading – this may become one of them. Steve Aisthorpe has written a tough and timely piece making a central contribution to the current and necessary re-imagination of Church.

He writes out of two loves. One is a love for the Church in her Jesus-centred, Spirit-enlivened, God-given identity. As a climber, and keen observer of nature, his other love is nature with her beautiful, complex interweaving of elements which, when allowed to flourish in rewilding, is diverse, sustaining and sustainable.

[Knowing the power of metaphors] he longs for and spells out what the re-wilding of the Church would mean, drawing parallels to ecological best practice. The agenda is not saving the Church as she is. Rather it is advocacy for diverse, risky communities of disciples to live and love following Christ, surrendering to the unpredictable Spirit. Then there is hope, as when wise rewilding occurs in nature, that the real Church will bounce back.

George Lings, researcher, thinker and author on mission and fresh expressions of Church

There are several times in the Bible where we are encouraged to see how God reveals himself in the natural world and in his Word – meaning both the Bible and ultimately his Son Jesus Christ. Steve Aisthorpe takes this encouragement seriously as he digs deep into the lessons we can learn from the land and ecology, from Scripture and from the call of Jesus that we should follow him.

In this fascinating and engaging book, Steve presents a compelling discourse that challenges and brings hope as we consider what God might be doing with his Church. This book was already important and timely before we experienced the global pandemic of COVID-19 and the total disruption of church life as we knew it. Now, even more, we need this book to spark our imaginations and send us back to the Bible and to the call of Jesus as we consider what it means to be his Church today and in the years ahead.

Elaine Duncan, Chief Executive, Scottish Bible Society

Writing in the shadow of the disruption created by COVID-19, Steve Aisthorpe highlights some key challenges facing today's church. Has Christianity lost its distinctiveness by prioritizing conformity and assuming that the divine Spirit operates only in ways approved by the institution? And what does it mean to be a Christian in this time and place? These and other provocative questions are explored here with honesty and empathy while also offering a vision rooted in the past in ways that can inspire a new future.

Revd Professor John Drane, educator and author

I have been gripped by the concepts of both rewilding and wilding for the last few years with regards to the natural world. An approach to change that loves the world, looks and notices what is happening and works with it, rather than operating out of a managerial mindset to get what you can out of it, is inspirational. And the results are dramatic in transforming the landscape. My heart leaps when that metaphor is applied to faith and church. It's evocative and opens up the imagination for so many possibilities. This is a book whose moment is now. Steve explores several aspects of rewilding and sets them in conversation with church, mission and faith in today's world. It's not a manual for what to do, more a set of instincts to nurture a whole different way of thinking and behaving. It is laced with practical wisdom from Steve's years of working with churches to help them navigate change. Let the rewilding begin!

Jonny Baker, Director of Mission Education,
Church Mission Society

Steve's book is a beautifully crafted story. It's a story that includes the Church but one that also transcends it. It's the story of our relationship with the natural world. This story not only challenges us to connect more deeply with the world around us but discerns a vision of what the Church can be. Steve sees an over-farmed Church that has lost its biodiversity, but he also sees a Church that is being called by the Spirit to return to the wild. So rather than mourning a declining Church, we're called to an awareness of and celebration of a Church set free, a Church that is returning to the wild.

Tim Nash, Pioneer Minister and Co-founder of
Nomad Podcast

If I had a difficult mountain ascent facing me, there's no one I'd rather have as my guide than Steve Aisthorpe. And having worked with him and read his first book, *The Invisible Church*, there are few others I'd rather have as a guide into the unknown territory of what lies ahead for the Church.

From the opening pages, the challenge is evident: 'The Christian Way has been domesticated and it is time to rediscover the adventure of faith.' In none of this is Steve concerned with the saving of the Church as an institution. Rather he points to following Jesus, a 'Wild Messiah,' wherever that leads, and always with an emphasis on the kingdom.

This is not a book for those who are looking for 'business as usual.' It's for those who are prepared to give way to the leading of the Spirit. It's for those who are prepared to 'pause, consider, pray' about where we're being called to.

Rt Revd Dr Martin Fair, Moderator of the General Assembly of the Church of Scotland

Steve Aisthorpe has written a highly readable, thoughtful and challenging meditation on the future of the Church, which abounds in grace, wisdom and evocative ecological parables and metaphors. This is a book full of insight and gentle provocation – which invites a contemplative reading and could be a good retreat companion for those taking time to reflect on prospects and priorities for their church.

Revd Dr Doug Gay, Principal of Trinity College, University of Glasgow

In this captivating and stimulating book, Steve Aisthorpe uses the concept of rewilding to challenge the contemporary church to put love back at the centre of its life and work. By a careful analysis of rewilding of agricultural landscapes, rooted in Scripture and supported by interviews with people who have stopped attending church, Steve draws out essential points to help shape the future of the Church, not least in a plea to re-centre ourselves as followers of Christ. The rewilding of the Church is a concept that challenges current approaches to mission, emphasising that love must be at the centre, so that innovation can take place at the edges. Although this book is not written for the rural church, or even from a rural perspective, it has particular relevance for all churches in rural areas. It is an important and timely book that speaks into the narrative on church growth.

Canon Dr Jill Hopkinson, Tutor in Rural Ministry, Sarum College, Salisbury; independent rural researcher and consultant

Rewilding the Church

Steve Aisthorpe

SAINT ANDREW PRESS
Edinburgh

First published in 2020 by
SAINT ANDREW PRESS
121 George Street
Edinburgh EH2 4YN

ISBN 9780715209813

First published in 2020
Second impression 2021

British Library Cataloguing in Publication Data

A catalogue record for this book is available from the British Library.

It is the publisher's policy to only use papers that are natural and
recyclable and that have been manufactured from timber grown
in renewable, properly managed forests. All of the manufacturing
processes of the papers are expected to conform to the environmental
regulations of the country of origin.

Typeset by Regent Typesetting
Printed and bound in the United Kingdom by
CPI Group (UK) Ltd

Contents

Acknowledgements

'Alone we can do so little. Together we can do so much.'[1] So said Helen Keller, a woman who learned to overcome her lack of sight and hearing by, among other things, developing an outstanding capacity to cooperate with others. The writing of this book has certainly been an exercise in collaboration. While I take full responsibility for what follows, a number of people have made invaluable contributions to both the thinking behind it and to the writing process. In particular I want to convey heartfelt thanks to John, Jon, Sue, Pete, Adam, George, Mike, Hilary, Lesley, Benjamin, Andrew, David, Grace and Stephen. Without their comments, questions, suggestions, encouragement and critique, this book would be much less than it is. Staff and Council members of the Mission and Discipleship Council of the Church of Scotland (now part of the Faith Nurture Forum) have not only allowed me the time to pursue research and writing, but have been enthusiastic and supportive throughout, as has Christine Smith and colleagues at Saint Andrew Press (Hymns Ancient and Modern). Dawn Martindale and Hannah Sanderson deserve special mention for their help with some of the research mentioned here. Many thanks also go to Diane Knowles, who generously used her time and eye for detail to provide an accurate set of references. Finally, love and thanks to Liz, John and Scott for all their encouragement and the numerous times they said, 'Keep going.'

---

1 Lash, J., 1980, *Helen and Teacher: The Story of Helen Keller and Anne Sullivan Macy*, New York, NY: Delacorte, p. 489.

Bible Quotations

OPEN: Read This First!

'I will put in the wilderness the cedar, the acacia,
the myrtle, and the olive;
I will set in the desert the cypress,
the plane and the pine together,
so that all may see and know,
all may consider and understand,
that the hand of the Lord has done this,
the Holy One of Israel has created it.'
Isaiah 41:19–20

Excellent. It's worked. I thought that if I called this page 'Introduction' many readers would skip over it. However, it's important, so please excuse me for luring you in by disguising it as the first chapter! A brief explanation of the kind of book you are reading will help you engage with it in a fruitful way.

An adventure begins

Rewilding the Church takes a recent idea in ecology and environmentalism as a metaphor for what God is doing in the Church. 'Rewilding'[1] is a radical strategy that allows natural forces to 'take the driving seat'. Advocates of rewilding argue that much of what is done in the name of conservation is little more than the preservation of man-made landscapes through human intervention and management. It's time, they assert, to step back and

---

1 The term 'rewilding' was first used by conservationist Dave Foreman, and was first refined and developed as a strategy for conservation biology in Soulé, M. and R. Noss, 1998, 'Rewilding and Biodiversity: Complementary Goals for Continental Conservation', *Wild Earth*, 8, pp. 19–28.

allow the processes within nature to reshape the environment. Where key species have been lost, they may be reintroduced. 'Invasive species', those that have no legitimate place in an eco-system and hinder its healthy development, should be culled or eradicated. Rewilding is a large-scale approach that recognises the importance of connectivity between habitats. It is a strategy that is provocative and contentious.

Rewilding the Church echoes the exhortation of Jesus to give thoughtful consideration to the ecosystems of which we are part: 'Look at the birds … consider the lilies'.[2] Jesus urged his followers to observe nature and to reflect on what they saw there. The Scriptures abound in metaphors and similes from the natural world. Our attention is drawn to the character, behaviour and interactions of certain species: 'Go to the ant, you lazybones; consider its ways'.[3] We are invited to con-template the verdant flourishing of a well-rooted riverside tree, fruitful even in times of drought, and find wisdom for our own choices and behaviour.[4] Instruction is offered on how to interact with the natural world, which, at the same time, offers allegories for life and faith and character.[5] Without the multitude of allusions to the natural world our Bibles would be threadbare and lifeless.

Rewilding the Church argues that our appetite to plan, man-age, contain and control has not only led to an environmental crisis, but has also disrupted the natural patterns in the Church. The same human instincts that have disrupted our natural environment have also constrained the Church. What began as a Spirit-empowered movement has become hindered by excessively complex and risk-averse institutions. The Christian way has been domesticated and it is time to rediscover the adventure of faith.

---

2 Matthew 6:26–34.
3 Proverbs 6:6.
4 Jeremiah 17:8.
5 For example, the concept of a sabbatical year in Leviticus 25 would prevent the depletion of soils, demonstrate God's faithful provision, including for those in need, during the fallow period.

A powerful metaphor

In the following pages we will explore some movements or actions for Christians, congregations and institutions to embrace. Together these comprise pathways towards the re-centring and refocusing of the Church on Jesus. God is rewilding the Church and wants to rewild you and me. The almighty Creator yearns to breathe new life into the 'dry bones'[6] of groups and congregations that feel weary and fragile. At the heart of the natural world there is a powerful capacity for regeneration and growth and at the core of the Christian community is an 'incomparably great power ... the same as the mighty strength he exerted when he raised Christ from the dead'.[7] Where the Christian faith has been reduced to something predictable and safe, we have stepped aside from the way of Jesus. But the wild Messiah refuses to be tamed. The One we follow is 'wild, dangerous, unfettered, and free'.[8]

In the time I have been writing this book, 'rewilding' has been the subject of constant media debate. It rarely makes the headlines perhaps, but is frequently lurking in the inside pages of newspapers. Conservation organisations that have for decades focused their resources on preserving man-made landscapes are switching their strategies towards letting natural processes shape the environment. Fans of *The Archers*, the BBC Radio 4 soap opera and the world's longest running drama, have been introduced to the idea, as Ambridge residents have debated the wisdom of allowing nature to have its way in the fields of Brookfield Farm. Inevitably the discussions that hit the headlines tend to be the extreme examples, where landowners seek to reintroduce long-extinct predators such as wolves and bears. However, behind these are exciting realisations in the natural sciences and new insights into the powerful processes and intricate interconnectedness of the natural world of which we are a part.

---

6 Ezekiel 37:1–14.

7 Ephesians 1:19–20 (NIV).

8 Brueggemann, W., 1998, *A Commentary on Jeremiah: Exile and Homecoming*, Grand Rapids, MI: Eerdmans, p. 138.

Like any metaphor, rewilding offers both points of connection or similarity and points of contrast or challenge. The
parables that Jesus told evoke a process of thinking and rethink-
ing and insight and action, not because they accurately describe
reality and not because they prescribe a particular response.
Rather, 'They draw the reader into their narrated world by
means of their narrative style, their proximity to reality, and
in particular, their figurativeness.'[9] Likewise, a good metaphor
engages the imagination, casting the familiar in a new light and
revealing the previously invisible or unconsidered. In discussing the merits of another metaphor, that of 'exile', the Hebrew
Scripture scholar Walter Brueggemann explains the dynamic
way in which a good metaphor operates: 'a metaphor proceeds
by having an odd, playful and ill-fitting match to its reality,
the purpose of which is to illuminate and evoke dimensions
of reality which will otherwise go unnoticed and therefore
unexperienced'.[10]

Rewilding the Church explores afresh the compelling
invitation of Jesus to 'Follow me' and the call to 'throw off
everything that hinders and entangles'.[11] It poses provocative
questions and offers signposts towards renewal. It comes into
your hands with the sincere prayer that it will inspire you to
think, pray, reflect and act in ways that will contribute to the
great rewilding of the Church – and of you.

Rewilding is a means rather than a specified end. In common
with rewilding approaches to the landscape, the chapters that
follow identify principles and approaches rather than any preconceived outcomes. In nature, when natural processes are
allowed to reign, a sustainable authentic landscape emerges; in
the Church, when our focus is on being the people Jesus calls
us to be, what emerges will be a living, growing, ever-changing
Church. We live in a time when the word 'crisis' is often applied

---

9 Zimmermann, R., 2015, 'Reader-oriented approaches: a playing
field for polyvalent parables', in *Puzzling the Parables of Jesus: Methods
and Interpretations*, Minneapolis, MN: Augsburg Fortress, p. 151.

10 Brueggemann, W., 1997, *Cadences of Home*, Louisville, KY:
John Knox, p. 2.

11 Hebrews 12:1 (NIV).

to both the environment and the Church, but there is a sense in which crisis is the Church's normal state, as it experiences the inevitable tension between its identity, calling and present reality. In the words of Dutch missiologist Hendrik Kraemer, 'The Church is always in crisis ... its greatest shortcoming is that it is only occasionally aware of it.'[12] The concept of rewilding is a lens that will bring our crisis into crisper focus and bring some paths towards renewal into sharper relief.

One Church, many manifestations

My use of a capital 'C' for 'Church' in much of this book is more than a matter of editorial style. If it is spelt that way the reference is to the whole Christian community, 'the body of Christ',[13] rather than to any particular organisation, institution or denomination. The Church is the 'one, holy, catholic and apostolic Church' referred to in the ancient Christian creeds. Where the lower case is used, the reference is to a local expression of this single Church. We live in times of increasing diversity in how the Church is manifested, from ancient and complex institutions to small informal groups and virtual networks. Indeed this growing 'biodiversity' is one indication of God's rewilding activity.

Pause and think about that

In the Hebrew text of the Psalms and Habakkuk there is a word which, despite occurring more than seventy times, is of uncertain meaning. In some translations it is simply omitted and in many it remains untranslated and is simply transliterated as 'selah'. The earliest Greek translation of the Hebrew Bible, the Septuagint, translated it as *daplasma* meaning 'a division'. Hippolytus, the second-third-century Christian theologian,

---

12 Kraemer, H., 1947, *The Christian Message in a Non-Christian World*, International Missionary Council, p. 24 (first published 1938).
13 1 Corinthians 12:27.

thought the term meant a change in rhythm or melody, a direction to musicians, singers or readers perhaps. Whatever the exact meaning, it seems likely that the author of these passages wanted the readers and listeners to pause and to pay particular attention; perhaps something along the lines of 'stop and listen' or 'pause and think about that' might be a contemporary equivalent.

The original manuscript for this book was punctuated with a series of text boxes containing questions for application, short prayers or suggestions for further reflection. However, on further consideration, it seemed like that style of presentation was inconsistent with the character and substance of the rewilding metaphor; it felt controlling or subtly directive. Rewilding involves a conscious decision to loosen control and to allow the forces of nature or the power at the heart of the Church freedom to shape what emerges. So, the text boxes have been replaced with regular reminders of *selah*: prompts to pause, to consider how you are responding to what you have just read, to ask in prayer whether anything is being provoked or inspired or challenged or encouraged in you personally or in regard to any group, congregation, network or denomination you are part of. These encouragements to reflect like this are accompanied by space within the text to allow you to make a note of anything of interest or significance for you.

As we begin to consider what might be triggered or inspired by our reflections on rewilding, let's pray together:

Almighty loving Creator, maker of beautiful biodiversity, founder and head of your Church, help me to engage with thoughts of nature and Church with a mind and a heart open to anything and everything you want to show and teach and do. In the name of the wild Messiah, Jesus, and in the life-giving, fear-quenching, power of your Spirit, rewild my soul and your Church. Amen.

2

LOOK: Rewilding? The Church?

'Look at the birds of the air ...
Consider the lilies of the field ...'
Matthew 6:26, 28

A new word, a new idea

The English language is growing. Despite having about a million words to choose from, users of English find it necessary to invent or develop about a thousand additions to our shared vocabulary each year. Continuous processes of linguistic evolution are at work. The decreasing usage of some words reflects the diminished place in our ever-changing culture of whatever they represent. Likewise, the appearance of new words reveals the emergence of new concepts and ideas. Prior to 2016, the word 'Brexit' meant nothing; 'vittles', once a common word meaning food, has disappeared from everyday usage and is now considered archaic, a quaint Victorian remnant.

A word that first graced the pages of dictionaries in 2011 is 'rewilding'. As happens with new-born words, its meaning continued to evolve. To begin with, it referred to the process of restoring an area of land to its natural uncultivated state. It became associated with the reintroduction of species of wild animals that had been exterminated in the past. In 2013 a widely acclaimed book entitled *Feral*, by environmental journalist and activist George Monbiot, suggested that rewilding 'is not an attempt to restore [ecosystems] to any prior state, but to permit ecological processes to resume'. Critiquing traditional approaches to conservation as seeking 'to manage nature as if tending a garden', he points out that much of what we cherish as natural landscape is actually a manmade desert compared to what would occur if the processes of nature were allowed to have their way. 'It is as if conservationists in the Amazon had decided to protect the cattle ranches, rather than the rain-forest',[1] Monbiot suggests. And so, in recent years, the term 'rewilding' has become the clarion call of a growing band of ecologists and environmental activists who assert that, rather than being seen as a collection of species, nature needs to be understood as the ever-shifting relationships among these species and their environment. In the words of Monbiot again: 'to keep an ecosystem in a state of arrested development, to preserve it as if it were a jar of pickles, is to protect something which bears little relationship to the natural world'.[2]

Now, you might well be thinking, 'This is all very interesting,' (I'm hoping so anyway!) 'but what has this got to do with the Church?' Well, I believe that the concept of rewilding offers a set of ideas with which we might better understand how we got to where we are as churches in the Western world and possible pathways to renewal. Several facets of the rewilding concept offer lenses through which we can better understand the complex challenges we face. But bear with me while we continue to develop our understanding of rewilding a little further.

Words such as 'unspoiled' and 'wilderness', sometimes applied to our national parks and nature reserves, suggest tracts of land fashioned by the forces of nature and home to the unbridled interactions of soil, vegetation, insect and animal life. However, the reality is invariably a situation where the environment's natural inclinations are muted and managed, constrained and controlled. Some processes are fostered and others are suppressed. While we might prefer to delude ourselves that it is otherwise, the environment is managed for our convenience and according to the preferences of landowners and policy makers. My own home, the Scottish Highlands, is a prime case in point; the grazing of vast swathes of upland by sheep and deer has created closely cropped hills, suppress-

---

1 Monbiot, G., 2013, *Feral: Rewilding the Land, Sea and Human Life*, London: Allen Lane, p. 8.
2 Monbiot, *Feral*, p. 9.

ing the regeneration of the native forest and its attendant ecosystems. Don't get me wrong. Nobody loves the scenery of the Highlands more than me, but the fact is that what we see is a seriously subdued version of the temperate rain forest that the forces of nature would create if unchecked. With 'the most concentrated pattern of land ownership in the developed world',[3] a small cadre of landlords have chosen to manage vast tracts of land in ways that best facilitate stalking, shooting and fishing. Their choices have produced the landscape we have learned to find picturesque – and therefore want to preserve.

Genuine wilderness has not existed in the UK on any substantial scale within living memory. This means that the 'baseline', the point of reference, by which landowners, decision-makers, and users of the countryside make comparisons and judgements, is something close to what we currently see. And we have learned to like what we see.

What advocates of rewilding suggest is that, rather than treating landscape as something to be preserved, leading to national parks which are more like Monbiot's 'jars of pickle' than unspoiled wilderness, we should allow the processes inherent to nature to do their thing. There are some notable examples of how, in some parts of the world, in relatively short periods of time, radically different landscapes and ecosystems emerge when human control is significantly diminished or ceased. Sadly, where rewilding has occurred most spectacularly it has rarely been the outcome of human decision. The most dramatic examples have often been the unintended consequences of conflict, environmental catastrophes or humanitarian crises and nobody is suggesting that these are desirable. For example, thirty years after a fire and explosion destroyed the Chernobyl Nuclear Power Plant in Ukraine, leading to the permanent evacuation of thousands of people from the surrounding areas, wildlife diversity and numbers were found to have increased

---

3 Jim Hunter, Emeritus Professor of History at the University of the Highlands and Islands, quoted in McKenna, K., 2013, 'Scotland has the most inequitable land ownership in the West. Why?', 10 August, *The Guardian*, www.theguardian.com/uk-news/2013/aug/10/scotland-land-rights (accessed 20.07.2019).

dramatically.[4] Surveys of mammal populations in the contaminated area, carried out by recording the tracks of certain key species from helicopters during times of snow cover, have shown steady increases of elk, roe deer and wild boar and that 'the relative abundance of wolves living in and around the Chernobyl exclusion zone site is more than seven times greater than in the four nearby uncontaminated nature reserves'. The conclusion that 'Humans are more damaging to wildlife and ecosystems than is radiation poisoning' adds support to arguments for rewilding as a radical strategy for reinvigorating the environment: when people surrender the driving seat to nature itself, the results are dramatic.

Another extraordinary example of rewilding has occurred in the Kočevje region, in the south of Slovenia, huddled against the Croatian border. Historically it was a region grazed by sheep and goats and as a result, 150 years ago, only about 30 per cent of forest cover remained. However, the human population of the area was relocated and dispersed – first by the Nazis, then by the Red Army and the communist government. It is now 95 per cent wooded. And not just scrub, but towering forests, inhabited by bears, wolves, lynx, wild boar, and the most incredibly rich diversity of wildlife of all kinds. Nobody is suggesting that biodiversity should be pursued through humanitarian crises. The point being made by advocates of rewilding who quote such examples is that when humankind releases its grip on the processes of nature, the potency and complexity of the renewal of life that occurs is truly remarkable.

Change and controversy

As an approach to the natural environment, rewilding is contested. Proposals to reintroduce high-level predators create

---

4 GrrlScientist, 2015, 'What happened to wildlife when Chernobyl drove humans out? It thrived', 5 October, *The Guardian*, www.the guardian.com/science/grrlscientist/2015/oct/05/what-happened-to-wildlife-when-chernobyl-drove-humans-out-it-thrived (accessed 04.04. 2018).

heated debates about both the risks and the benefits. As I sat down to write this chapter, BBC radio reported a passionate dispute related to the proposed reintroduction of the Eurasian lynx to the Kielder Forest in Northumberland. The chief scientific adviser at The Lynx Trust, quoted in the national newspapers, makes moral and economic arguments for allowing these magnificent creatures to occupy the apex of the local food chain: 'Lynx belong here as much as hedgehogs, badgers, robins, blackbirds – they are an intrinsic part of the UK environment … We killed every single last one of them for the fur trade, that's a wrong we have to right.'[5] Meanwhile, opposition from sheep farmers is equally ardent, with claims that livestock would be put at risk. Representing the interests of local farmers, the Chief Executive of The National Sheep Association predicts public outrage at 'harrowing images' resulting from 'distressing attacks' and argues that 'our countryside now is far too fragmented and built up to support a viable population of lynx'.[6]

Rewilding, whether it's the environment or the Church, is a means of change and change will always be contentious. Changes to the status quo inevitably mean different things to different people. Practical implications vary and emotional responses even more so. Those of us involved in accompanying church congregations through journeys of change know that, in many ways, 'change' is the easy bit. 'Transition', the psychological process people go through to come to terms with change, is the difficult part. For most people, change is perceived as a loss before it is experienced as a gain. We cannot, therefore, initiate a process of change without creating a grief reaction in people – however irrational this may sometimes seem. Neuroscientists assure us that fear and excitement are

5 Carrington, D., 2017, 'Lynx could return to Britain this year after absence of 1,300 years', 7 July, *The Guardian*, www.theguardian.com/ environment/2017/jul/07/lynx-could-return-to-britain-this-year-after-absence-of-1300-years?CMP=fb_gu (accessed 27.07.2019).

6 Baynes, C., 2017, 'The lynx could be reintroduced to the UK within months after a 1,300-year absence', 10 July, *The Independent*, www. independent.co.uk/news/uk/home-news/lynx-1300-years-reintroduced-uk-kielder-forest-a7832036.html (accessed 27.07.2019).

exactly the same in terms of brain chemistry, but that is of little help to those caught up in the emotional whirlwinds that can be roused by changes to our familiar environment – whether ecological or ecclesiastical. Let's be clear, rewilding means change, change means transition, and transition is never an easy ride.

My usual advice to church leaders is that, when initiating any kind of change, whether small or huge, 'communicate, communicate, communicate ... and when you think that you have communicated enough, communicate some more'. The conventional wisdom is to communicate a picture of the future, to cast a vision; communicate the purpose of change and the reasons for change; communicate clearly regarding the part that people have to play; communicate in every possible way and many times. But rewilding is not conventional. If we can communicate the new future then it is not rewilding. By definition the rewilded future is unknown. We cannot convey a vision or an outcome. Rather, we must convince people of the integrity of the process.

We need to get used to change. That will be the new norm. Following Jesus brings change. As his followers and apprentices we will be changed continually from the inside out. As agents of his kingdom, we will be catalysts of change. For any group or community with Jesus at its centre, change is integral, fundamental, to be expected. When Jesus expounded the characteristics of the kingdom he did so through stories, sketching out principles, but never prescribing a destination. The principles are constant; their outworking and impact in an ever-changing context are unpredictable. This is a genuine adventure; some might prefer the term 'wilding' to 'rewilding', since, far from reverting to some previous state, rewilding is a journey into an unknown and unpredictable future.

Selah

Time to consider and pray?

Open your eyes

Jesus did not tell us, as many translations suggest, just to *look* at the birds and *consider* the lilies. The words he used literally mean 'fix your eyes on these things' or 'take a really good look'. Commenting on these passages in Matthew's Gospel, Bible scholar and keen ornithologist the late John Stott writes '... he meant more than that we should notice them ... the Bible tells us that birds have lessons to teach us'.[7]

The fact that the natural world has so much to show us and teach us in relation to our Christian walk and life together would have been patently obvious until recent decades. However, the sad truth is that what was clearly evident for many centuries needs to be restated and clarified today: the 'works of the Lord' that the Scriptures instruct us to study, and take delight in,[8] include creation. It should not need saying. A straightforward reading of the Bible makes the meaning clear, but in some Christian traditions passages that speak of 'the works of the Lord' are understood to refer only to God's acts of redemption.

Tragically, the theology of creation has been much neglected. Indeed it is worse. In addition to widespread disregard, there has sometimes been positive suspicion or even fear regarding looking to nature as a source of revelation and inspiration. For some, to be too concerned with the natural world whiffs of pantheism, a view that eliminates any distinction between God and his creation and sees everything as part of an all-encompassing, immanent God. Such a fear has, it seems, led to the disposal of baby and bathwater together and a view of nature as a distraction rather than a source of insight and understanding. It was not always the way, it has rarely been the way, and it should not be the way. To ignore the role of nature in forming and informing our faith is at best ungrateful, at worst sacrilegious.

---

7 Stott, J., 1999, *The Birds, Our Teachers: Essays in Orni-Theology*, Oxford: Candle Books, p. 9.

8 Take Psalm 111:2 for example: 'God's works are so great, worth a lifetime of study – endless enjoyment!' (MSG).

Referring to the Sermon on the Mount, the German reformer Martin Luther wrote, 'You see, he is making the birds our schoolmasters and teachers ... Whenever you listen to a Nightingale, therefore, you are listening to an excellent preacher.'[9] John Wesley, the eighteenth-century reformer to whom is attributed the rule of life 'Do all the good you can, by all the means you can, in all the ways you can, in all the places you can, at all the times you can, to all the people you can, as long as you ever can', still considered it time well spent to write an extensive two-volume tome, *Survey of the Wisdom of God in the Creation*.[10]

From the Desert Fathers such as Anthony of the Desert (c.251–356) to the thirteenth-century theologian Thomas Aquinas (1224–74) to the contemporary Franciscan theologian Richard Rohr, there is a rich seam of wisdom which views the natural world as 'a second book' from which, along with the Bible, we can learn and be changed into greater Christlikeness. Francis Bacon, the philosopher and 'father of the scientific method', was quoted to this effect in the opening pages of Charles Darwin's *On the Origin of Species*: 'To conclude, therefore, let no man out of a weak conceit of sobriety, or an ill-applied moderation, think or maintain, that a man can search too far or be too well studied in the book of God's word, or in the book of God's works; divinity or philosophy; but rather let men endeavour an endless progress or proficience in both.'[11] And this idea of 'two books' of revelation has a basis within the pages of the Bible too. Take a look at the pair of psalms we know as Psalm 103 and 104. The first is a passionate celebration of God's gracious acts of salvation and his faithfulness in keeping his covenant with his people:

---

9 Luther, M., 1521, *The Sermon on the Mount*, translated by Pelikan, J., Vol. 21 of *Luther's Works*, Saint Louis, MI: Concordia, pp. 197–8.

10 Wesley, J., 1823, *A Survey of the Wisdom of God in the Creation*, New York, NY: N. Bangs and T. Mason.

11 The passage is from Bacon's 1605 book *Advancement of Learning* and is quoted within the title pages. Darwin, C., 1859, *On the origin of species by means of natural selection, or the preservation of favoured races in the struggle for life*, London: John Murray.

'Bless the Lord, O my soul, and do not forget all his benefits – who forgives all your iniquity, who heals all your diseases, who redeems your life from the Pit.'[12] The second is an equally enthusiastic outpouring, but focused on how God's majestic character is revealed and reflected in the rich biodiversity and complex inter-relationships within the natural world: 'Bless the Lord, O my soul ... You make springs gush forth in the valleys; they flow between the hills, giving drink to every wild animal; the wild asses quench their thirst. By the streams the birds of the air have their habitation; they sing among the branches. From your lofty abode you water the mountains; the earth is satisfied with the fruit of your work. You cause the grass to grow for the cattle, and plants for people to use.'[13]

My theological education taught me to view the ways in which God reveals himself as divided into two categories: 'special revelation', centred on the incarnation and the canon of Scripture, and 'general revelation', comprising the ways in which God has made signs of his presence and character available to everyone, regardless of their knowledge of Jesus and the Bible. General revelation, and in particular creation, the natural world, was rightly presented as secondary in terms of clarity and fullness. And yet, there is a sense in which both in history, and in the lived experience of individuals, the natural environment is prior to any special revelation. Addressing Christians in Rome, Paul wrote, 'For what can be known about God is plain to them, because God has shown it to them. Ever since the creation of the world his eternal power and divine nature, invisible though they are, have been understood and seen through the things he has made.'[14] Before the incarnation, before a word of Scripture was penned, God's handiwork in creation made his presence and power 'plain to all'. Facing a crowd of pagans in Lystra trying to worship him following the healing of a lame man, Paul explained that this had not been his own doing, but was a sign from 'the living God, who made the heavens and the earth and the sea and everything

12 Psalm 103:2–4.
13 Psalm 104:1, 10–14.
14 Romans 1:19–20.

in them' and who had 'not left himself without testimony: he has shown kindness by giving you rain from heaven and crops in their seasons; he provides you with plenty of food and fills your hearts with joy'.[15] Paul pointed the people, first of all, to what they knew and experienced: God's generous provision through the remarkable and bountiful processes and seasonal cycles that facilitated their agriculture. In the words of Richard Rohr, 'Creation is our first and final cathedral. Nature is the one song of praise that never stops singing.'[16]

The birth of a blind spot

Close to my home, surrounded by hundreds of acres of Scots pine, larch and birch, is a compact constellation of Guinness-black pools. Uath Lochans are kettle hole lakes, formed where huge hunks of ice calved from the snout of the retreating Spey Glacier. They are echoes of an entirely different era.

Clustered as they are at the foot of the Cairngorm mountains, an area renowned for its ferocious winds, it is remarkable how often these deep peaty pools take on a mantle of utter stillness. At such times, the inky skin of these ancient pools is taut and motionless. Until, that is, my dog jumps in! And then, throughout the rest of our time there, the treacle-like surface swells and wrinkles. Waves and ripples gradually traverse the surface, fanning out and out, eventually lapping upon and licking every inch of the bank.

Visiting this precious place recently I began to reflect on how, sometimes, events create waves that ripple down through the ages. Happenings in eras far beyond living memory and even beyond recorded history continue to impact us. Their echoes may be faint, but their influence is undeniable. I think that one such event took place at Streoneshalh. No, it is not a typing error. The unfamiliarity of the name reminds us that what took place there belongs to an era largely forgotten. Streoneshalh

---

15 Acts 14:15–17 (NIV).

16 Rohr, R., 2011, 'Nature and the Soul' in *Radical Grace*, Summer, 24(3), Cincinnati, OH: St Anthony Messenger Press.

was the name given to the place where, in AD 664, a gathering of church leaders made decisions which still influence us now.

Perched on a cliff top, 199 steps above the town of Whitby, hanging over the very edge of England's eastern seaboard, the remnants of Streoneshalh (also known as Whitby Abbey) still point heavenward. Today the evocative Gothic remains are best known as the inspiration for Bram Stoker's *Dracula* and Whitby is heralded as the 'Goth capital' of Britain. However, the convocation that occurred here more than a dozen centuries ago was of altogether greater significance and has shaped our perceptions in subtle but important ways ever since.

Streoneshalh was the home of a 'double monastery' (that is, linked monasteries for women and men, where they lived separately but worshipped together), overseen by its founder and Abbess, Hild (later to be Saint Hild). The historian Bede, a contemporary of Hild, records that this was a community of love, peace and charity, where all property and goods were held in common, the Scriptures were studied and acts of service were performed with generosity and joy.[17] Clearly Hild herself was held in high esteem and there are accounts of other church leaders and kings coming to her to seek advice. So it was here in AD 664 that King Oswiu of Northumbria convened the assembly later known as the Synod of Whitby.

At that time, whereas most parts of what is now the British Isles were dominated by one Christian tradition or another, in Northumberland two great traditions met and mixed. Here Christians following the Ionan way, a tradition within 'Celtic Christianity', coexisted with those more closely associated with the Roman Church. Superficially, at least from our perspective of considerable hindsight, it seemed that the agenda of the Synod of Whitby was another example of the Church's inclination to indulge its own trivial pursuits.[18] The main agenda

17 *Historia ecclesiastica gentis Anglorum* (Ecclesiastical History of the English People) was written by the Venerable Bede in about AD 731 and recorded the history of the Church in England around that time.

18 Robin Greenwood, a visiting Fellow at Durham University, once commented in a book with a title remarkably similar to the one in your hand that 'For the majority of people in this country our churches are irrelevant, peripheral and seemingly only concerned with their

items for this monumental assembly were how to set the date for celebrating Easter and rules and practice related to 'tonsure', the custom of cutting or shaving the hair on the head as a sign of devotion. However, as the outcome of the Synod would be closer alignment with one tradition over another, there was more at stake. Now we can look back and trace certain changes within the Church to having their origins in choices made in that clifftop convention.

The emergence of an indoor religion

It would be naïve and factually inaccurate to portray the events at Whitby as Celtic Church versus Roman Church; a tradition that viewed attention to the natural world as integral to the life of faith being subjugated by a more institutional model. There was no such coherent, independent Celtic Church. Also, in addition to the great strengths of that tradition which have stimulated a resurgence of interest in things 'Celtic' in recent years, there was also plenty that many contemporary Christians would want to distance themselves from. In our enthusiasm to seek out pre-Christendom models of church to guide us through the challenges of our post-Christendom world, there is sometimes a danger of creating a stereotypical Celtic church which is more of an idealised notion than an historical reality. Also, within the Roman tradition there were those who recognised the natural environment as something to celebrate, study and learn from. What can be said, however, is that the Church's interest in and connection with the earth's natural processes moved during this period from being intuitive to becoming something of a blind spot.

As the influence of Rome increased and the traditions associated with the Celtic Church held less sway, Christianity in the north moved from being an outdoor religion to an indoor one. Creation became less important in terms of doctrine and Christian practice. Ray Simpson has studied the life and mission

---

own trivial pursuits.' Greenwood, R., 1988, *Reclaiming the Church*, London: Collins, p. 156.

of Aidan, the prominent leader within Celtic Christianity who passed away just thirteen years before the Synod of Whitby. Reflecting on the contrasting perspective and attitudes towards the natural environment during Aidan's lifetime and what came after Whitby, he notes that '... the Christianity introduced by the Roman mission ... was an indoors religion. Once they were baptised, people had to leave their farmsteads and come to an unnatural, ornamented building called a church.'[19] Simpson sees a rift between the land, the natural environment and their faith as originating in the adoption of Roman traditions and suggests that this has been deepened and reinforced in recent centuries by cultural changes such as rationalism, industrialisation, individualism and consumerism. Aidan and his contemporaries 'could not have envisaged a time when Christians would make no connection between the Jesus who saves individuals from their sins and the Jesus who sustains creation' Simpson suggests. Others argue this point even more strongly. Harold Massingham, the prolific writer on all things rural, reflecting on the relationship between faith and ecology, and considering the influence of the Synod of Whitby, states that 'If the British Church had survived it is possible that the fissure between Christianity and nature, widening through the centuries, would not have cracked the unity of Western man's attitude to the universe.'[20]

We should be grateful then that more recent international assemblies have begun to redress the balance within the Church's conceptualisation of mission and we should hope that the influence of these will percolate through the whole. The worldwide Anglican Communion's mission statement, for example, recognises the intimate and inextricable relationship between the Church's commitment to 'proclaim the good news of the Kingdom' and 'to strive to safeguard the integrity of

---

19 Simpson, R. and B. Lyons-Lee, 2016, *St Aidan's Way of Mission: Celtic Insights for a Post-Christian World*, Abingdon: Bible Reading Fellowship, p. 48.

20 Massingham, H. J., 1943, *The Tree of Life*, London: Chapman & Hall, p. 40.

creation and to sustain the life of the earth'.[21] In Scotland the ecumenical organisation Eco-Congregation Scotland is raising awareness and encouraging Christians to understand the link between environmental concern and Christian faith.[22] The Christian charity A Rocha, inspired by the biblical mandate to care for the earth, is encouraging churches to work for the restoration of the natural world, campaigning on biodiversity issues, and has initiated the Eco Church across England and Wales.[23] The World Council of Churches has highlighted the fact that issues of justice, peace and environmental protection are inseparable.[24]

Although the Church's awareness of it has ebbed and flowed, nature is abounding in inspiration and plenteous in wisdom. American author and assiduous observer of nature Annie Dillard articulates well the tragedy of our sometimes inattention: 'Beauty and grace are performed whether or not we will sense them. The least we can do is try to be there ... so that creation need not play to an empty house.'[25] It is providential that at a time when the Church is in urgent need of renewal, the concept of rewilding has gained prominence. Rewilding as an environmental approach reminds us that the hope for our fragmented and increasingly threadbare landscape lies not in humankind's abilities to intervene and manage, but in the powers and processes of nature itself for regrowth and diversification. Here is a pertinent parable for the Church in the early twenty-first century. The renewal of the Church will come from the inside out as we refocus on following Jesus together, allow his Spirit to re-form us, and listen for his guidance with open minds and obedient hearts.

As enthusiastic as I am about the environment, the purpose of this book is not to raise further awareness and stir interest

---

21 The Lambeth Conference adopted 'Five Marks of Mission' in 1988 and they were then adopted by the General Synod of the Church of England in 1996.

22 www.ecocongregationscotland.org.

23 www.ecochurch.arocha.org.uk.

24 www.oikoumene.org.en.

25 Annie Dillard, in Yancey, P., 2001, *Soul Survivor*, London: Hodder & Stoughton, p. 221.

in biodiversity and the health of our landscape. As utterly convinced as I am that care for the earth is an integral aspect of our vocation as apprentices of Christ and participants in God's mission, the intention here is not to further highlight or expand on that. Rather, the following chapters take a concept from ecology and find within it a powerful metaphor for the renewal of the Church. That concept is rewilding.

Selah

Pause. Reflect.

The people and the land

It is sometimes assumed that the habit of Jesus to use imagery from the natural world was simply a matter of familiarity and relevance to his original hearers, an example of good communication skills. Again and again, speaking with farmers and fishermen and housewives, he drew attention to the tools of their trades, the fruits of their labours, the competences and challenges of their particular livelihoods. His favoured images were not imaginary. They were important and integral aspects of their seasonal undertakings, the warp and weft of life. These people knew the miracle of life contained in the tiniest seed, the capacity of weeds to spoil, the difference a well-tilled soil could make to the health or hunger of their family. That soil was under their fingernails and engrained into the soles of their feet as he spoke. Time and again Jesus encouraged them to see how the familiar scenes of their daily lives spoke of God's ways, how the tools and the context of their working day gave insights regarding the plans and purposes of God. Throughout the Gospels we find Jesus instructing his followers to 'look!', 'see!', 'open your eyes!'

For those who see Jesus' enthusiasm for pointing his hearers to nature as just good practice by making connections with what was familiar to his hearers, the assumption is that, were he to be making the same points in the contemporary Western world, he would draw his illustrations from technology or the world of entertainment instead. However, for Jesus, the natural environment was not just a source of imagery with which to illustrate his point. He was drawing on and building upon the strong links within the Hebrew Bible between God, his people and the land. The recurring theme of 'the land' in God's dealings with his people is not simply a matter of territory. Again and again we find powerful interdependent connections between the wellbeing of the natural environment, the security and health of the people, and the depth and fidelity of the people's walk with their God. Old Testament scholar Chris Wright explains the framework of ethics within the Hebrew Scriptures in terms of a relational triangle with God, the people and the land at the three apexes.[26] 'The land in which Israel lived ... was not merely the place where they happened to live ... [nor] merely an economic asset ... The land ... was of central theological and ethical importance.'[27] The diverse books of the Old Testament, history, poetry and law alike, speak with one voice regarding the centrality of the wellbeing of the natural environment and its inextricable link with the faithfulness of God's people. Biblical leaders such as Solomon, Ezra and Nehemiah implore the Lord to heal and restore the land as they seek forgiveness on behalf of the nation. Prophetic visions of God's blessing and ultimate purposes for his people envisage times when people live in harmony with the natural world. The Psalms brim over with hymns of praise which see God's blessing as synonymous with land that is fertile, well-watered and productive and a wider natural order which speaks of God through its beauty, diversity and provision for humankind. Russ Parker, writing in the context of pastoral care and the Christian ministry of healing, points out that within the almost 3,000 biblical references to the land we are encouraged to recognise a direct connection between the

---

26 Wright, C., 1984, *Living as the People of God: The Relevance of Old Testament Ethics*, London: IVP.

27 Wright, C., 2010, *Old Testament Ethics for the People of God*, London: IVP, p. 76.

human story and the ecological context in which that story occurs: 'In challenging the people of God to seek forgiveness and healing for their sins, God promises to forgive those sins and, much more, to heal their land.'[28]

If our concern is for the renewal of the people of God, we are well advised to open our eyes to our environment and the processes within it. Indeed, the term 'ecology' actually has its roots in two of the most important words of the New Testament. 'Eco' comes from *oikos*, a word often translated into English as 'household'. In the Christian Scriptures, in addition to meaning a physical house or the extended family associated with a particular home, a concept that was considerably wider than blood relatives, it is also used as an important metaphor of belonging for the emerging Christian community. Although the suffix 'logy' has been used for several centuries to refer to the study of something (e.g. geo*logy*, theo*logy*, bio*logy*), its origins (or etym*ology*!) are in the Greek word *logos*. That's the word we find in the opening phrase of John's Gospel: 'In the beginning was the *logos*' – and again, a few verses later, in the astonishing statement, 'The Word (Logos) became flesh and lived among us, and we have seen his glory, the glory as of a father's only son, full of grace and truth.'[29] *Logos* was a word coined by Greek philosopher Heraclitus to refer to the divine reason or wisdom at the heart of the universe. Six centuries later, John took immense care in choosing the words with which to enlighten his eclectic audience regarding the incarnation of the Creator. Logos, he decided, suited his holy purpose. Much later, when the word *ecology* appeared on the scene it was to describe 'the study of communities'.

In the world of the New Testament the concept of a household was less founded on kinship than on relationships of dependence and subordination. It was an economic unit of up to a hundred people rather than a family in the modern sense. A person was included in the household because of their relationship to the *pater familias*, the head of the household, who

---

28 Parker, R., 2012, *Healing Wounded History: Reconciling Peoples and Healing Places*, London: SPCK, p. 8.
29 John 1:14.

exercised authority over the whole *oikos*. What we easily fail to grasp as we read the New Testament through our twenty-first-century Western eyes is that Jesus and the apostles introduced a radical reconfiguration of the concept and practice of family and household. So, for example, when Jesus pointed to his disciples and said, 'Here are my mother and my brothers'[30] he was inferring a fundamental reconstituting of the family. A new *oikos* was emerging, established not on the headship of a senior patriarch, but based on the relationship of people with God. Hence Jesus' words, 'For whoever does the will of my Father in heaven is my brother and sister and mother.'[31] This new family, with God as its head, is the embodiment of the radical inclusion taught by Jesus and his followers. When we read the New Testament carefully we see that social barriers are crashing down. Paul, sometimes wrongly accused of misogynistic tendencies, was at pains when writing to the believers in Rome to choose gender neutral language to emphasise that, in contrast to prevailing customs in the surrounding society at that time, inheritance within this new family was not dependent on gender.[32] Historians who have studied the development of the early Church have noted how the *oikos* was the nucleus for the burgeoning Christian community.[33] Again and again we find greetings in the Epistles to the believers associated with particular households.[34]

Oikos and *logos*. Considering this background, it is hardly surprising that ecology should provide fruitful metaphors and insights for the Church. Indeed, how could a rift ever open up between ecology and theology?

---

30 Matthew 12:49.
31 Matthew 12:49.
32 Romans 8:17.
33 For example, Green, M., 1970, *Evangelism in the Early Church*, Grand Rapids: MI, Eerdmans, pp. 207–23.
34 For example, the houses of Prisca and Aquila (Romans 16:5), Stephanas (1 Corinthians 16:15) and Onesiphorus (2 Timothy 1:16).

Pathways to renewal

Cornwall has some of the most sublime scenery in the UK. The mountains and glaciers of the Alps comprise some of the most exquisite jewels in the environmental crowns of France, Austria, Italy and Switzerland. However, the euphemistically named 'Cornish Alps' tell a tragic tale of carelessness for nature and stand as a stark reminder of mankind's willingness to sacrifice ecosystems for profit. Scattered around the old market town of St Austell, on what was previously granite moorland, the extraction of kaolin, or china clay, for the production of porcelain and paper has left a bleak ravaged landscape. For every ton of china clay removed approximately nine tons of mineral waste has been extracted, creating a moonscape of deep lesions in the land.

It is here, in the midst of this environmental catastrophe, this egg box-like scenery of peaks, pits and lagoons of clay slurry, that Dutch-born British businessman Tim Smit conceived the idea of constructing the outstanding environmental education venture known as The Eden Project. Visitors who enter this one time industrial wasteland are confronted by two gigantic domes, each constructed of hundreds of hexagonal plastic cells supported by miles of intricate metal framework. The larger dome, 55 metres tall, simulates a tropical rainforest environment; the second dome, slightly smaller, but still enormous, replicates a Mediterranean environment. In the middle of the former, were it not for the wheelchair-friendly pathway, it would be easy to imagine oneself in a remote corner of Costa Rica or Borneo. I for one was grateful to make use of the refrigerated 'Cool Room' before continuing to revel in this incredible replica of a tropical 'biome'. But, it is a replica. Although The Eden Project uses the term 'biome' for these two massive structures, that term is more correctly used of something that exists on a whole other scale.

Biomes are biological communities that have formed in response to a shared physical climate. They comprise a vast multitude of interwoven habitats. Clearly, on one level, the contents of the carefully controlled bubbles of climatic conditions of The Eden Project are the real thing. Within the four acres of the so-called 'Tropical Biome' hundreds of species of trees, plants and animals, all normally found somewhere between the Tropics of Cancer and Capricorn, are living side by side. The genetic credentials of each organism are faultless. On one level it is indisputably 'real'. However, there is, of course, nothing like the complexity of interactions or the soils built up over centuries and millennia that exist in a genuine tropical rainforest. There is some wonderful wildlife, but a tiny selection. Most visitors would not appreciate the full range of creepy crawlies; the Health and Safety Executive would not look favourably on the presence of some of the more deadly reptiles and larger predators. The fact is that it is real, but not authentic. It is a little bit wild, but not really wild. It is meticulously planned and rigorously regulated. It is a piece of tinned rainforest, hermetically sealed from its temperate surroundings.

And what about our churches? Are they authentic, the real deal? Are they communities that emerge out of the work of God's Spirit in the lived faith of his people? Are they, as previous Archbishop of Canterbury Rowan Williams has suggested, 'what happens when people encounter the Risen Jesus and commit themselves to sustaining and deepening that encounter in their encounter with each other'?[35] In asking such questions I am not querying the reality of people's faith. I do not doubt the good intentions of church leaders. I am certainly not questioning the undeniable fact that God is at work in and through church congregations and the lives of so-called 'churchless Christians'. I am, however, suggesting that in our well-meaning efforts to create, facilitate, organise, manage and control, we are sometimes in danger of surrendering authenticity for mere reality. By having an image of what a good church might be and working towards that end, we easily sacrifice an expression of church that arises from a genuine encounter of the gospel with the people whom God is drawing together. By creating and maintaining congregational models that require certain functions and roles, we forgo a community that emerges

---

35 Cray, G. (ed.), *Mission-shaped Church*, London: Church House Publishing, 2004, p. vii.

from the gifts of its people, shaped by the context of their lives and the realities of the wider community. The distinction I am making may seem obtuse or subtle, but it is certainly important. It is the difference between a community with Jesus at its heart and a club for followers of Jesus. In one we are firmly in control; the other is the result of our surrendering the driving seat. One is the parallel of traditional conservation and George Monbiot's 'jar of pickles', the other is rewilding.

Selah

Take a moment. Think. Pray.

But where to start? Reflecting on the revolutionary nature of Jesus' call to all who will follow, Brian McLaren writes, 'The uprising begins not with a strategy but with a new identity. So he spurs his hearers into reflection about who they are ...'[36] Rewilding the Church begins by drawing from the deep wells of Christian identity.

---

36 McLaren, B., 2014, *We Make the Road by Walking*, London: Hodder and Stoughton, p. 160.

3

IDENTITY: Who Do You Think You Are?

'You are Christ's body – that's who you are!
You must never forget this.'
1 Corinthians 12:27 (MSG)

Who do you think you are?

It is a compelling format. In its sixteenth series at the time
of writing, each episode of the BBC television series *Who Do
You Think You Are?* traces the ancestry of a celebrity. With
some expert assistance, long-buried secrets are unearthed. The
fortunes of forgotten family members are full of surprises.
A politician discovers ancestors of dubious moral standing.
Within the family tree, legacies of oppression and injustice
come to light. A celebrated actor finds among his ancestors a
man who, like himself, had a passion to perform. His spirits
soar as it emerges that this great uncle got his first big break
in the very same town as he did. Then he is distraught to find
that whereas his own career in film and theatre has led to fame
and prosperity, for his great uncle the uncertain life of even
a successful actor in that era had taken a cruel twist and saw
his predecessor end his foreshortened days in the workhouse.
While the variety of backstories in each series of the show
is vast, every participant, without exception, recognises that
discovering 'who they are' changes them.

Who we think we are really matters.

In his book *Awareness*, the Indian Jesuit priest and psy-
chotherapist Anthony De Mello retells a fable in which a
poultry farmer finds an eagle's egg and puts it under a broody

hen.[1] The eaglet hatched and grew up with other newborn chicks and their mothers. All his life the eagle did what the other chicks did. It scratched at the ground for worms and insects. Occasionally it would flap its wings and fly a few feet into the air before returning to earth and continuing to rummage for grubs. Years passed and the eagle grew old. One day it saw a magnificent bird circling in the sky above. This splendid creature glided gracefully, rising effortlessly in a column of rising air with scarcely a single beat of its glorious golden wings. The aged, earthbound eagle gazed up in awe and asked, 'Who is that?' 'That is the king of the birds, the eagle,' replied a neighbour, the wonder and reverence clear within its voice. 'It belongs to the sky. We belong to the earth. We are chickens.'

Who we think we are really matters.

The salt of the earth, a letter from Christ, a chosen race, a holy nation, the people of God; the faithful, the sanctified, the justified; a new creation, the first fruits, the new humanity, the bride of Christ[2] ... the list goes on. In his seminal work *Images of the Church in the New Testament*, Paul Minear explores in some depth ninety-six distinct metaphors, but also points out that there are more.[3] Just as the meticulously planned and precision-cut facets of a diamond ensure the maximum return of light to the viewer, the New Testament provides us with multiple windows into the complex and glorious reality that is the Church, the body of Christ, the flock of the Good Shepherd, God's fellow workers[4] (as I said, the list goes on).

Who we think we are really matters.

---

1 De Mello, A., 1992, *Awareness*, New York, NY: Image Books/Doubleday.

2 Many of these images are repeated in different books of the New Testament and by different authors, but here is a sample in the order that they appear in the text above: Matthew 5:13; 2 Corinthians 3:2–3; 1 Peter 2:9; 1 Peter 2:9; Romans 9:25–26; Colossians 1:2; 1 Corinthians 1:2; Romans 3:26; 2 Corinthians 5:17; James 1:18; 1 Corinthians 15:20–23; Ephesians 5:22–31.

3 Minear, P., 2004, *Images of the Church in the New Testament*, Louisville, KY: Westminster John Knox.

4 Romans 12:5; John 10; 1 Corinthians 3:9.

One of the optimum ways to cut a diamond is into the complex multifaceted shape known as the 'modern round brilliant'. Its fifty-eight surfaces optimise the stone's 'brilliance', its capacity to reflect light. But there is more. The intricate multidimensional geometry of a skilfully cut gem also enhances its 'dispersive power', its ability to split white light into its component spectral colours. From the lips of Jesus and from the quills of Paul, Peter, James, John and others, we are furnished with a plethora of perspectives on, and metaphors for, what we generally call the Church. Each provides a crucial and inspiring insight into our self-identity. Taken together they form an image that is incredibly rich and multidimensional. Indeed we find the authors themselves of the New Testament often struggling to contain themselves and yet also fighting to find adequate expressions to communicate the wonder of it all: 'No eye has seen, no ear has heard, and no mind has imagined what God has prepared for those who love him.'[5] At times their reasoned explanations and arguments just have to be set aside while the writer indulges in an outpouring of adoration: 'For from him and through him and to him are all things. To him be the glory for ever. Amen.'[6] The glory and the gratitude are just too much. Worship is the only adequate response: 'Now to God who is able to strengthen you according to my gospel and the proclamation of Jesus Christ, according to the revelation of the mystery that was kept secret for long ages but is now disclosed, and through the prophetic writings is made known to all the Gentiles, according to the command of the eternal God, to bring about the obedience of faith – to the only wise God, through Jesus Christ, to whom be the glory for ever! Amen.'[7]

Who we think we are really matters.

Within the Bible's enthralling and electrifying portrait of the Church, certain core themes can be identified. First of all, a personal connection between God and his people is highlighted. It is difficult to imagine, for example, a more intimate and vital linkage than between head and body. Second, the images of

---

5 I Corinthians 2:9 (NLT).
6 Romans 11:36.
7 Romans 16:25.

Church depict a radical new society, where love rules, walls of division are broken down, diversity is welcomed and yet unity is absolute. Third, numerous images remind us of the purposes of the Church. God's mission and the work of Christ continue and the Church is to participate in the family business. To follow Jesus is to be both an apprentice and an accomplice. We are fashioned and gifted for our particular involvement. We are collaborators with him in the work of redeeming creation. Each member of the body, equipped and being shaped by God, brings a unique and crucial contribution to this shared task. Finally, the Bible's tapestry of metaphors makes it clear that the Church is *en route* to something much more. It is in transit towards a glorious future. What we see now is but a preliminary glimpse, a foretaste of a future which is superior to anything we can imagine. It is this latter characteristic of the Church that Hans Küng, the Swiss theologian, had in mind when he described the Church as '... essentially an interim Church, a Church in transition, and therefore not a Church of fear, but of expectation and hope; a Church which is directed towards the consummation of the world by God'.[8]

Who we think we are is important. And metaphors matter. In the case of the Church, they are powerful shapers of our self-understanding.

Who are you and why are you here?

Shortly after the death and resurrection of Jesus Christ, an influential rabbi by the name of Akiva ben Yosef lived in Capernaum. This fishing village on the northern shore of the Sea of Galilee had been the home of Simon Peter. It is where Jesus called his first disciples and where he healed many people. Akiva was a prominent figure in the religious scene of his day. He made a major contribution to the *Mishnah*, the important collection of Jewish oral traditions, and was a supporter and friend of Gamaliel, the most distinguished rabbi in Jerusalem

---

8 Küng, H., 1967, *The Church*, London: Burns and Oates, p. 131.

and teacher of Saul of Tarsus whom we now know as Saint Paul.[9]

The story goes that Akiva was ambling along the edge of the water one day. The day was almost over. The light was fading into the dusky half-light of evening and Akiva, caught up in his meditations, missed his turning and wandered on to the wrong path. Still contemplating a particular passage in Isaiah, instead of coming upon the gate of Capernaum he found himself in front of the local Roman garrison where he was stopped in his tracks by the brusque bark of a young sentry on the wall above: 'Who are you and why are you here?'

Following the rabbinic tradition, the rabbi responded to the question with one of his own: 'How much do they pay you to stand guard and ask that question of anyone who approaches?' No doubt the young sentry was a little taken-aback by Akiva's retort, but realising that the intruder was a rabbi who constituted no threat to the fortress, he replied: 'Five drachma a week'. The rabbi then made the young man an offer: 'I will pay you double that if you will come and stand in front of my home and ask me that question at the beginning of each day.'

Akiva knew the paramount importance of knowing one's identity and purpose – and our tendency to forget these most fundamental details. Lack of clarity about who we are and why we are here is at the root of much confusion, dispiritedness and angst regarding the Church. One of the primary challenges we face as Christians, as followers of Jesus Christ, is to hold on to a clear sense of who we are and our calling, our *raison d'être*. When we consider who we become when we embrace the gracious invitation of Jesus to 'follow me', we are overwhelmed with awe and wonder. Little wonder, then, that the extraordinary, mindboggling, barely conceivable identity of those who are 'in Christ' is a dominant theme in the writings of the apostle Paul. Over 150 times he uses phrases such as 'in Christ' and 'in the Lord' as he tries to fathom the depths

---

9 Acts 22:3. The Acts of the Apostles also records how Gamaliel intervened with wise and persuasive words at the trial of the apostles: Acts 5:33–40.

and grasp the heights of the astonishing privileges and benefits conferred on every follower of Jesus Christ.

We are a 'new creation', no longer under any kind of condemnation, recipients of 'the incomparable riches of God's grace', citizens of a kingdom characterised by grace, joy and peace for ever.[10] Paul explains that, before we benefited from all Christ achieved on our behalf, we were 'far away' from God, but now we are 'brought near', welcomed into the very presence of almighty God. In fact, the word Paul employs to describe our journey from estrangement to reconciliation was a term used in the context of ushering someone into the royal court. It implies the granting of access to the most privileged position.

It reminds me of the celebrated photograph of President J. F. Kennedy in the Oval Office of the White House with his son, John Junior, playing under his desk. The fascination of the picture stems from the contrast between the most powerful man on earth, sitting in a place that symbolises great authority, and the simple, trusting play of a child. Others, even powerful politicians, influential admirals and great generals, would only ever enter that space for a particular purpose and with clear authorisation. Even then they never got to play! John Junior, however, was there, hanging out and having fun, because the Commander-in-Chief was his dad. Since the day when, as Jesus died, 'the curtain of the temple was torn in two', the barrier restricting access to the most holy place rent 'from top to bottom',[11] we are permanently welcome in the royal court of the King of kings. Jesus encourages his followers, as they approach this King of kings, to stand in his sandals and to remember and embrace their identity as beloved sons and daughters: 'This is your Father you are dealing with, and he knows better than you what you need. With a God like this loving you, you can pray very simply. Like this: Our Father in

---

10 These comprise just a tiny taster and can be found in 2 Corinthians 5:17, Romans 8:1, Ephesians 2:7, Ephesians 2:13, 1 Timothy 1:1, 14, Philippians 3:20.

11 Matthew 27:51.

heaven ...'[12] As leading New Testament scholar N. T. Wright explains, the Lord's Prayer is 'an invitation to share in the prayer-life of Jesus himself'. Exploring this thought further, Wright goes on to explain that the follower of Jesus is 'incorporated into the inner life of the triune God' and 'intended not just to believe that this is the case, but actually to experience it'.[13]

Clearly, although they were a little slow on the uptake in the early days of their journeying with Christ, the first followers of Jesus came to grasp and experience the awe-inspiring and astounding privilege they inherited as his disciples. The reader of the epistles of Paul, Peter, John and others is drenched and almost overwhelmed by a tidal wave of metaphors and similes which struggle to express the realities of life 'in Christ'. In any other sphere of life the language marshalled by the writers of the New Testament would be dismissed as extravagant exaggeration. However, when employed in expressing the blessings that God has lavished on his children, even the highest hyperbole can never adequately capture the inexpressible reality.

Even just for starters, you are God's beloved child, a friend of Jesus Christ, justified, united with the Lord, bought at a price, a member of Christ's body, chosen, adopted, redeemed, forgiven; you have direct access to the throne of grace, you are free from condemnation and you cannot be separated from God's love; God will complete the good work he started in you because you are a citizen of heaven; you are a branch of Jesus Christ, the true vine, and a channel of his life, chosen to bear fruit; you are God's temple, an ambassador of the King of kings and so, so much more.

Selah

Hmm ... Time to pause.

---

12 Matthew 6:8–9 (MSG).

13 Wright, N. T., 2001, 'The Lord's Prayer as a paradigm of Christian prayer', in Longenecker, R., *Into God's Presence: Prayer in the New Testament*, Grand Rapids, MI: Eerdmans, pp. 132–54.

Spiritual amnesia

So we are the recipients of the most utterly remarkable grace. We are part of something that takes our breath away when we pause to consider it. And yet we forget! It seems that we suffer from a strange kind of forgetfulness. We hear and embrace these most staggering truths. Glimpses of our identity 'in Christ' leave us reeling and awestruck. And then ... we forget. Our attention span for things divine, our functional memory when it relates to those truths we claim as of paramount importance, is curiously stunted. As Eugene Peterson, author of *The Message*, has observed, 'Having been introduced to God, we soon lose interest in God and become preoccupied with ourselves. Self expands and soul atrophies. Psychology trumps theology.'[14] Long before the high-tech distractions of the current era, John Donne was able to confess his irresistible tendency to forget his maker at the slightest or most subtle distraction: 'I neglect God for the noise of a fly, the rattling of a coach, the creaking of a door.'[15]

Many of our efforts to cultivate a devotional life are aimed at nurturing an awareness of our true identity. As we engage in spiritual disciplines, the ancient practices of engagement (such as prayer, fellowship, study and celebration) and the lesser known practices of abstinence (such as solitude, silence and fasting), we are reminded of who we are and the life purposes that are inherent in that. We engage in 'holy habits'[16] in order to counter the 'atrophy of the soul', to foster a more consistent awareness of who we are in Christ and to invite the Spirit of Christ to form and grow his character within us. We participate in 'discipleship' activities to seek what has been

---

14 Peterson, E., 2013, *Practice Resurrection: A Conversation on Growing Up in Christ*, Grand Rapids, MI: Eerdmans, p. 56.

15 Quoted in Yancey, P., 2002, *Reaching for the Invisible God*, Grand Rapids, MI: Zondervan, p. 201.

16 Andrew Roberts's book *Holy Habits* (2016, Welwyn Garden City: Malcolm Down) and associated study materials explore ten habits mentioned in Luke's description of the early Church in Acts 2: biblical teaching, fellowship, breaking of bread, prayer, giving, service, eating together, gladness and generosity, worship and making more disciples.

described as 'a God-ward transformation ... a lifelong, whole-life reorientation which will have challenging implications for our self-identity, our belonging within community, our belief systems and our daily behaviour'.[17] Akiva ben Yosef recognised the vital significance and transformational potential of knowing the answer to the young watchman's question: 'Who are you and why are you here?' If we have resolved to be faithful followers of Jesus and if the health of his Church is of concern to us, we need to do likewise.

We need to allow the metaphors of the Church to shape our self-understanding; we need to allow the work of God's Spirit to form his character within us. Without this ongoing renewal we tend to fall into one of two traps with regard to the Church. One mistake is to see it only as a human institution, a kind of religious club; the other is to venerate it to such an extent that it becomes the focus of our interest and energies at the expense of a devotion centred on its founder and head himself. When the former becomes our perspective, when the Church is viewed as no more or little more than an organisation, then, in a society where most institutions are defined by markets or entertainment value, we begin to understand the Church and our relation with it in those terms. When this perception of church holds sway, despite it being disguised in spiritual language or churchy jargon, churches end up competing for market share and people's attention. Success is measured by 'attendance' and what is celebrated as 'church growth' is often the unintentional recruitment of people by one church from another.

The second snare, the risk of esteeming Church and seeing it as the object of our dedication and devotion, is the opposite extreme of the first. Just as our perspective can be deformed or diluted by thinking too little of the Church, equally our self-understanding can be distorted by too high a view of Church. Having just been reminded of the overflowing wonderment of the New Testament authors in relation to Church, it may

17 Anglican Consultative Council, 2016, *Intentional Discipleship and Disciple-making, An Anglican Guide for Christian Life and Formation.*

seem strange now to suggest that we might ever be in danger of considering the Church too highly. Surely, if the Church is so central to the plans and purposes of the almighty Creator, even the highest view is in danger of underestimation? However, as paradoxical as it may seem, the risk is the same as the first danger. Both fail to recognise the pre-eminence of God himself. Seeing the Church purely as the result and arena of human activity fails to adequately recognise God as the Church's creator, Jesus as its head and the Spirit as the One who inspires and animates its life. Perhaps more subtle, deceptively pious in appearance, but equally effective in deforming and twisting our self-understanding, is a veneration of the Church over Jesus himself.

The Church's founder and the source of its life and meaning is both human and divine. In his body, the Church, the handiwork of God and the sometimes wonderful, sometimes flawed, endeavours of his people are intertwined, both shaping the realities we see and experience. Just as our Saviour is both human and divine, so is his body, the Church.

A concept of Church distorted by too low an understanding, that emphasises the human over the divine, tends to create unloving critics. An adoration of Church that surpasses and displaces a devotion to the Lord himself disposes us to an uncritical love of Church for its own sake and we become blinded to its very real flaws. The Church already has plenty of unloving critics. It has enough uncritical lovers too. What it can always use is some loving critique.

With these potential deceptions in mind, as we seek to understand the Church and pursue its renewal, we need to move beyond the question of *who* we are, and consider the even more crucial matter of *whose* we are. In academic language, Christology is previous to ecclesiology; our understanding of Jesus should shape our understanding of Church. A focus on *whose* we are fosters an awareness that first and foremost we are 'beloved by God'. It is in the gaze of his inestimable love that we hear the call 'follow me' and embark on the adventure of faith. When we understand ourselves as first and foremost loved by God, other facets of our identity find their proper place. When that core element is lacking we find ourselves constantly striving to build self-worth by other means. In his book *Abba's Child*, the American writer on spirituality Brennan Manning shares some wise advice: 'Make the Lord and his immense love for you constitutive of your personal worth. Define yourself as one beloved by God. This is the true self. Every other identity is illusion.'[18]

It is out of the recognition and acceptance of our 'belovedness' that we both create and become part of a new community, with Jesus as its head and with love as its hallmark and touchstone. As the Dutch priest and theologian Henri Nouwen wrote in *Life of the Beloved*, 'To be chosen as the beloved of God is something radically different. Instead of excluding others it includes others. Instead of rejecting others as less valuable, it accepts others in their own uniqueness. It is not a competitive, but a compassionate choice.'[19] The role of metaphor in informing and evoking our self-identity is vital. The power of spiritual disciplines to form our character is unique. Rewilding the Church begins here: knowing ourselves to be beloved, putting our roots down deep into Christ, allowing our self-identity to be reshaped in the light of Scripture, discerning his purposes and stepping out into the adventure of faith.

How did we get here?

In her book *Forgotten Girl*,[20] Naomi Jacobs describes the terrifying experience of waking up from a nightmare drenched with sweat. Flabbergasted, she discovers that she is not in her childhood room, where she feels sure she had gone to sleep the previous night. Why is her sister not lying in the top bunk above her? Indeed, where *is* her bunkbed? Instead of waking

18 Manning, B., 1994, *Abba's Child: The Cry of the Heart for Intimate Belonging*, Colorado Springs, CO: Navpress, pp. 49–50.

19 Nouwen, H., 2002, *Life of the Beloved: Spiritual Living in a Secular World*, New York City, NY: Crossroad Publishing Company, p. 55.

20 Jacobs, N., 2015, *Forgotten Girl: A Powerful True Story of Amnesia, Secrets and Second Chances*, London: Pan.

under her familiar pink bedspread, she finds herself in a king-size bed in a room she has no recollection of ever seeing before. Has she been kidnapped during the night? Imagine the utter confusion, the sheer terror. But Naomi's account is not fiction and nor is it horror. Her book is the autobiography of someone who went to bed as a thirty-two-year-old mother and, through a rare condition known as Transient Global Amnesia, experienced a loss of nearly two decades' worth of memory, effectively catapulting her back into the mind of her fifteen-year-old self.

In *The Invisible Church*,[21] I described my own experience of coming back to Scotland after twelve years living in South Asia and the disorientating shock of realising how many people had disengaged from local churches during that period. Observing that phenomenon, combined with a realisation that the dramatic haemorrhage of churchgoers had often gone almost unnoticed, is what provoked me to undertake the research which underpins that book. However, the changing shape of the Christian community, with a large and increasing proportion of Christians not engaged with a local congregation, was only one aspect of the changes within the Church which disturbed me at that time. While less traumatic than Naomi Jacobs's wakening, it was tremendously perplexing and took some years to begin to understand what had occurred. The Church has experienced a substantial change to its self-understanding. Self-identity has been eroded.

In fact, 'erosion' is a good word in this context, because whereas Transient Global Amnesia happens overnight, the Church's loss of confidence or disorientation has been a more gradual though nonetheless forceful process. To use a different metaphor, there is a sense in which the Church has lost its bearings. It has become less certain in what it knows, but also in what can be known and how it can be known. The dramatic numerical decline in church attendance is easy to measure and relatively straightforward to evaluate, but along with that has

---

21 Aisthorpe, S., 2016, *The Invisible Church: Learning from the Experiences of Churchless Christians*, Edinburgh: Saint Andrew Press.

been a deeper and more fundamental loss – and that is considerably more difficult to articulate, quantify and evaluate.

In the previous chapter we mentioned the idea of shifting 'baselines': how the point of reference by which we assess changes in the countryside moves over time; how we tend to evaluate changes in relation to our own limited experience rather than considering a longer-term view. So part of our struggle in identifying what has happened in the Church is our tendency to compare our experience with a baseline set within our own memory. We evaluate our experiences now with what we have known previously or elsewhere. In terms of the life of the Church, our baseline tends to be positively recent. To understand what has happened within our lifetime, we need to look back much further.

How did we get here? How did the revolutionary, counter-cultural, Jesus-inspired movement that burst on to the political and religious scene of first-century Palestine become what we know as the Church? Why is it that, while the radical Christian insurgency that erupted after Pentecost sent shock waves in all directions, the Church at the beginning of the twenty-first century is often seen as irrelevant, peripheral to society, a quaint relic of a bygone era? How did the Spirit-empowered community, centred on an utterly transformative message, become so domesticated? I winced recently when I read the words, '... too many parish churches become ghettos for those who wish to cling on to an archaic, monocultural ritual'.[22] It sounds harsh, but there is truth there. And it is not just 'parish churches' either. The congregations of denominations and networks may practise different rituals and their culture may be very different to the stereotype of a parish church, but there is a widespread malaise which is no respecter of theology or style.

As Ezekiel faced a valley full of dry bones the Lord posed the question, 'Mortal, can these bones live?'[23] Today, as we look at the Church, we often find ourselves making a similar

---

22 Simpson, R. and B. Lyons-Lee, 2016, *St Aidan's Way of Mission: Celtic Insights for a Post-Christian World*, Abingdon: Bible Reading Fellowship, p. 64.

23 Ezekiel 37:3.

enquiry of the Lord. Confronted by denominations that have become mired by wearisome bureaucracy we wonder whether it is possible to refocus our attention and energies on Jesus, to rediscover our first love and reignite a passion for living whole-heartedly for him. Encountering indifference as congregations haemorrhage members or apathy in the face of unchallenged injustices, we long for the life-giving breath that filled the early followers of Christ with a passion for sharing his love with others that eclipsed any concern for their own lives.

The gospel is still good to go

Of course while, as a broad generalisation, it is true to say that the Jesus movement of the first century was subversive and dynamic and that today it has become hindered by excessively complex institutions, there are sufficient exceptions to prove the proverbial rule. On a global level there are vast regions where the statistics of numerical growth in church attendance are beyond our wildest imaginings. Take the small Himalayan nation of Nepal for example. It is a place that is close to my heart and of which I have first-hand experience, having lived there for most of the nineties and noughties. This previously Hindu kingdom has experienced exponential church growth. From a small handful of persecuted believers in the 1950s, the Operation World website now estimates more than 850,000 Christians.[24] When a horrific earthquake struck that nation in 2015, the Christian community played a pivotal role in both the initial rescue response and the relief and rebuilding efforts that followed – something that would have been unimaginable just a decade or two earlier. And of course there are numerous similar stories from other areas in Asia, as well as parts of Africa and South America. The gospel, the same ancient message of forgiveness and reconciliation – the good news which promises freedom from the past, purpose in the present and hope for the future – is as potent as ever. The resurrected Christ is still in

---

24 www.operationworld.org.

the business of transformation. The wind of the Spirit is still bringing new life to barren places.

On our own doorsteps too, the gospel that Paul was convinced had the power to bring freedom and wholeness continues to renovate hearts, renew lives and create vibrant and transformative communities. Most areas of the Western world have church congregations that are vibrant and growing. The 2016 Scottish Church Census found that over 500 congregations reported significant numerical growth over the previous five years. The census also recorded about 300 new churches since 2002, about two-thirds of these planted by smaller denominations and independent groups. South of the border, the fresh expressions movement has had a significant impact over the past ten years. A careful study of developments within twenty-one Church of England dioceses found that these new kinds of Christian community comprised as many as 15 per cent of churches in these areas.[25] Perhaps most significantly, about 33 per cent of the people engaged with these communities had no previous church involvement and 27 per cent were Christians who had re-engaged after a period of non-engagement. So, in contrast to the widespread tendency for expanding congregations to grow at the expense of other congregations, a large proportion of people affiliated with these new expressions of Church are 'new Christians' – what church growth specialists refer to as 'conversion growth', as opposed to 'transfer growth' or the 'biological growth' of children from Christian parents being inducted into church congregations through the traditional routes of Sunday Schools and youth groups.

Whereas there used to be a widespread belief that the hundreds of thousands of people who have disengaged from local church congregations were no longer practising Christians or were at best on a steep and slippery slope of 'backsliding', we now know that this is not the case. Recent studies following up the research that underpinned *The Invisible Church* shows that most of the Christians interviewed in 2013–14 continue to

---

25 Lings, G., 2016, *The Day of Small Things: An Analysis of Fresh Expressions of Church in 21 Dioceses of the Church of England*, Church Army, pp. 87–8.

report that their faith is of central importance to them. A few have re-engaged with traditional congregational expressions of the Church, but most have not. Most are in fellowship of some kind; some are exploring new expressions of Church. As we sift the data of research from the community of so-called churchless Christians, another exciting flash of light that gives a glimpse of God's rewilding of the Church is the substantial number of people who report that they are Christians who have never been part of a traditional congregation. It was an exciting surprise when 15 per cent of churchless Christians recruited for the *Investigating the Invisible Church* study in 2014 reported that they had discovered the Christian faith and decided to follow Jesus but had never been regular church attendees.[26]

While there are countless signs of the gospel at work, stagnation and decline in church institutions is widespread. However, a rewilding of the Church has begun. The kingdom uprising that began at Pentecost may have been domesticated in modern times, but inside this pussy cat that we call the Church is a lion that strains to break free! What Martyn Atkins has identified within the Methodist Church as a 'holy yearning' and a 'divine disquiet'[27] I recognise in churches across Scotland. There is a stirring within Christians of many denominations and none. Having worked with many dozens of local churches over the last decade I know that they invariably include faithful, prayerful, committed people who have an intense ache, a craving for a deepening of personal faith, a thorough renewal of their congregations and a profound impact in their communities.

Having interviewed and surveyed hundreds of Christians who are no longer engaged with a local congregation in the traditional sense, I know that for many of these people an important aspect of their detachment from congregational

---

26 Aisthorpe, S., 2014, 'A survey of Christians in the Highlands and Islands who are not part of a church congregation', *Rural Theology*, November 12(2), pp. 83–95.

27 Atkins, M., 2010, *Discipleship ... and the People Called Methodists*, Peterborough: Methodist Publishing, www.methodist.org.uk/down loads/pubs-intra-discipleship-120710.pdf.

life is a desire for more than they were finding through their involvement with a local church: more in terms of their own encounter with God and personal transformation and more in terms of Christian concern for friends, neighbours and the wider community. One of the great surprises of the research summarised in *The Invisible Church* was the strong evidence of missional concern among church-leavers and the examples of new expressions of Church coming into being through the witness of post-congregation believers.[28]

This is not another 'how to' book on church. The litany of ecclesiastical self-help resources does not require further additions. Working with local congregations week by week as a coach, adviser and facilitator, I am painfully aware of the widespread weariness and wariness in the face of the multitude of tools and techniques for church renewal and congregational development. And yet, at the same time, there is an intense hunger for genuine change. There is a longing for a deeper experience of God and a more authentic encounter with one another.

Increasingly, in my personal reflections and in the conversations I have week by week with Christian leaders and local congregations, I find myself wondering: What if the pathway towards such a transformation is not about doing more, but less? What if it is not about the usual culprits, the faithful few, the enthusiastic minority, making plans and leading the way? What if it does not require extra resources of time or money or talents? What if it is more about releasing than managing? What if, instead of trying to grow and develop church, we focus on following Jesus, being the people he wants us to be, and see what happens?

Selah

Pause. Pray.

---

28 Aisthorpe, S., 2016, *The Invisible Church: Learning from the Experiences of Churchless Christians*, Edinburgh: Saint Andrew Press, pp. 167–83.

Moving beyond 'saving the church'

We live in exciting times. In Julian Barnes's novel *The Sense of an Ending*, the protagonist, Tony Webster, remembers, 'Someone once said that his favourite times in history were when things were collapsing, because that meant something new was being born.'[29] That describes well the current situation of the Church across the Western world in the early twenty-first century. And 'rewilding' is an incredibly helpful metaphor for what is already beginning to happen and what needs to happen. Something huge is going on. For some years figures for attendance and membership and other indications of involvement or affiliation with most long-established denominations have been plummeting in the most extraordinary way. There has been and continues to be a kind of institutional freefall. And yet when we have listened to the people who lie behind these statistics, by far the majority are clear that their Christian faith continues to be the mainspring of their lives. They are not leaving Jesus. Rather, in most cases, they are leaving the kind of organisational expressions of Church to which they were previously committed. And in most cases their departure occurs after many years of dedicated involvement.

While there are congregations that thrive by growing their market share of the declining cohort of people committed to traditional models of being Church, there is an increasing recognition that God is doing something new. There is a realisation that, rather than fighting for survival, there is a need to step back and discern what God is doing. In the widespread decline and the various bright sparks beyond the institutions, there is a sense that the Spirit of God is at work, challenging the followers of Christ to rediscover their identity, re-centre their lives on Jesus, and refocus their priorities. Our ideas of what it means to be Christian are being challenged. A rediscovery of

---

29 Barnes, J., 2012, *The Sense of an Ending*, New York, NY: Vintage, p. 105.

the 'Upside-Down Kingdom'[30] is turning our understanding of church and Christian practice on its head.

In recent decades, despite some helpful rediscovery and re-emphasis of the Church's place in the mission of God,[31] the focus has tended to remain on 'saving the church'. Attractional strategies and seeker-friendly tactics have sought to entice the not-yet-Christian into the congregation. However, we now find that even those who were previously leading advocates of 'missional church' increasingly recognise that adding 'missional' or any other modifier to 'church' is in danger of missing the point by yet again turning the focus back to the Church. Alan Roxburgh, a leading missiologist and author of, among other titles, *Introducing the Missional Church* and *The Missional Leader: Equipping Your Church to Reach a Changing World*, reflecting on the focus on reorienting churches around mission now suggests that 'it was a mistake because it became a conversation about saving our story called church'. His perception is that 'What's happening is a massive unravelling of our church story. There is no putting that story back together.'[32]

The time has come for a fundamental re-centring. Not a re-emphasising of any particular aspect of our calling and not a managing of congregations into particular configurations or styles. Rather, a rediscovering of our faith from the foundations up. If that sounds radical, then that is appropriate, as the word 'radical' is derived from a Latin word meaning 'of or having roots'. In the case of our Christian faith our foundation is not something structural and it is not achieved by renewing our commitment to any particular set of propositions. Rather, it is relational. We are to be rooted in a person. As Paul put

---

30 The term 'Upside-Down Kingdom' was coined by Donald Kraybill in his award-winning classic of that name (1978, Harrisonburg, VA: Herald Press).

31 Neatly summed up in the statement, 'It is not the church of God that has a mission in the world, but the God of mission who has a church in the world.' Dearborn, T., 2013, *Beyond Duty: A Passion for Christ, a Heart for Mission*, CreateSpace, p. 2.

32 Quoted on *Path of Renewal Blogspot*, 4 February 2017, retrieved 29 July 2019.

it in his letter to the followers of Jesus who lived in Colossae, 'Let your roots grow down into him, and let your lives be built on him.'[33] It is time to return to the simplicity of responding to that gracious invitation 'follow me' and to learn afresh to do just that, both as disciples and as part of his body. As one writer paraphrases Paul's exhortation:

> My counsel for you is simple and straightforward: Just go ahead with what you've been given. You received Christ Jesus, the Master; now live him. You're deeply rooted in him. You're well-constructed upon him. You know your way around the faith. Now do what you've been taught. School's out; quit studying the subject and start living it![34]

Renewal in an age of hunger

The call to a renewal from the inside out and with an open mind about what the Church that emerges will look like is nothing new. However, it has often been drowned out by well-meaning and powerful voices announcing the latest initiative to save the Church. As Bishop John Taylor pointed out in the 1980s, the Church, intended to be a Spirit-filled, Spirit-led community, has a strong tendency to settle into a framework of structures and procedures and then develop self-protective mechanisms for survival.[35] Reflecting on his work, Alison Morgan, in her own call for renewal, *The Wild Gospel*, writes, 'Taylor called for us to resist the pressure to settle for conformity and instead to learn to trade traditions of the church for the dreams of its people – not to reject or condemn the church, for the church is us, but to coax it into renewal ...'[36]

I like that phrase 'to *coax* [the Church] into renewal'. We seek, through our own wholehearted and ongoing 'yes' to

---

33 Colossians 2:7 (NLT).
34 Colossians 2:6–7 (MSG).
35 Taylor, J., 1986, *A Matter of Life or Death*, London: SCM Press.
36 Morgan, A., 2004, *The Wild Gospel: Bringing Truth to Life*, Oxford: Monarch, p. 278.

Christ's invitation, to seek renewal of ourselves. At the same time, as we journey with others (for our faith is profoundly relational and rarely if ever individual), we do what we can to urge, coax and encourage the body of which we are part to find its faithful expression. It is a task requiring much wisdom and abundant grace. To do this with integrity, to do it and not to be squashed by the weight of all that has gone before, to do it and not be constrained by the expectations of others nor inhibited by the concerns that naturally attend all adventures of faith, requires God-given courage and immense love. If grace is lacking, the best-willed efforts towards renewal become little more than church bashing. Our love for Christ, for one another and for the communities of which we are members need to be greater than our love for any institution.

Our traditions are a rich inheritance. They are deep wells from which to draw, but they must never become restraining anchors or limiters of holy imagining. When the Spirit is blowing we need to be prepared to cast off, raise the sails and commit to a journey towards an unknown destination. Henri Nouwen, drawing a parallel to Jesus' prayer for his disciples as ones who were 'in the world but not of the world',[37] writes of the difficulty of being in the Church and not of it in the sense of church itself taking centre stage:

> Being of the Church means being so preoccupied by and involved in the many ecclesial affairs and clerical 'ins and outs' that we are no longer focused on Jesus. The Church then blinds us from what we came to see and deafens us to what we came to hear.[38]

Rewilding the natural environment involves stepping back and allowing the inherent processes of nature to do their thing – rather than managing it towards some predetermined blueprint. It is the exact opposite of intensive agriculture. It is profoundly different to the preservation of manmade landscapes that characterise many 'conservation' efforts. Rewilding

37 John 17:16.
38 http://henrinouwen.org/meditation/being-in-the-church-not-of-it/.

the Church involves a refocusing on following Jesus and, together with others, allowing the unpredictable wind of the Spirit to guide and empower, to make us more who he knows we are. We do not endeavour to do a new thing simply because yesterday's ways are past their 'best before' date. However, we will find ourselves doing a new thing because God is always doing a new thing. Our Creator is still creating. Our calling is not to be attenders or consumers, but to be accomplices of Jesus, partners with God. The Church will be renewed because we are renewed and the Church is us.

The Church's malaise has sometimes been diagnosed as a disconnection from culture. However, our vocation is not to find accommodation with culture, but rather, like Christians of every previous generation and culture, it is to faithfully allow the gospel to engage with culture and participate in what emerges. Rewilding the Church is less about advocating a recoupling with culture and more about a reconnecting with Jesus and with each other. The identities of Church and individual disciple and Jesus are inextricably intertwined; 'discipleship is not something the Church does; it is what the Church is'; 'the plural of disciple is Church'.[39] We live in a time when spiritual hunger is approaching famine proportions. There is incontrovertible evidence that the number of people who identify themselves as 'spiritual but not religious' is rising. Often distained as 'fuzzy fence-sitters',[40] 'self-indulgent, narcissistic individualists'[41] or worse, such people share the same spiritual longing as many within churches. Churches perceived as standing for certainty, dogma and fixed practices are no place for pilgrims, but when

---

39 Morgan, A., 2015, *Following Jesus: The Plural of Disciple is Church*, ReSource.

40 Aune, K., 2014, 31 July, 'Belief without Borders: Inside the Minds of the Spiritual but not Religious, by Linda A. Mercadante'. Retrieved from www.timeshighereducation.co.uk/books/belief-without-borders-inside-the-minds-of-the-spiritual-but-not-religious-by-linda-a-merca dante/2014785.article (accessed 15.09.2015).

41 Daniel, L., 2013, *When 'Spiritual but not Religious' is not Enough: Seeing God in Surprising Places, even the Church*, Nashville, TN: Jericho Books.

Church is understood as what emerges from an open-hearted journeying with Christ, we will find many fellow travellers.

Let the rewilding commence.

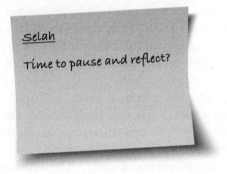

Selah

Time to pause and reflect?

4

FOLLOW: Reintroducing the 'Great Interferer'

'... they were terrified. But he said to them,
"It is I; do not be afraid."'
John 6:19–20

Follow me

When viewed from the valley on a benign spring day, the snow-blanketed whalebacks of the Cairngorm mountains seem to float on the horizon, the essence of tranquillity. On such a day it is difficult to imagine that these high granite plateaux host some of the most vicious weather on the planet. Here, the UK's highest wind speed was documented at 173 mph, shortly before the meteorological instrument recording the wind's speed was destroyed by its irresistible power. In such conditions nobody survives. Even at wind speeds a fraction of that extreme, snow and grit are whipped up into a terrifying maelstrom. Such whiteout conditions are suffocating, the air snatched away before you can inhale. Communication is barely possible. Visibility is restricted to your boots. Navigation and progress become a savage battle.

Some years ago I was running winter mountaineering courses. On one particular day serious climbing was out of the question, but the near-blizzard conditions offered an excellent opportunity to practise navigation skills and experience a taste of full-on winter turmoil. Hunkered behind a large cairn, having set a compass bearing, I cupped my hands against the thunderous roar of the wind and bellowed into client David's ear, 'FOLLOW ME'.

Staggering out into the open plateau, battling one violent gust after another, counting paces, compass in hand, I focused on stumbling in the right direction and, after a short while, squinted round the edge of my hood to check on David. Expecting to see him tucked in tight behind me, revelling in the meteorological mayhem, my heart sank when my glance was met by a wall of white. No David. Just a whirling tumult of airborne snow and ice, lashing and pummelling. If David was wandering around the plateau, his prospects were not good. Resetting my compass I staggered back towards the cairn and, probably just a minute or two after leaving, lurched into the relative protection of its leeward side ... and bumped into David. 'YOU JUST DISAPPEARED!' he yelled.

Following someone you can't see is really tricky!

But that is our vocation, both individually and together. The compelling invitation of Jesus, 'Follow me', is where it all begins. It is his initiative that makes our response possible and necessary. It is the calling into being of the Church. The positive response of disciples in every era, those who say 'yes' to that simple summons, constitutes the continuing establishing of the Church. And the invitation is ongoing. Consider the insight we get into his relationship with Peter, the ongoing nature of the summons to follow and the profoundly different implications that Peter must have known at different times. When he first heard the call of Jesus by the shore of Lake Galilee he accepted *without hesitation*.[1] By the time the same words of Jesus formed part of their post-resurrection conversation, the invitation was the same but also radically different. Peter's eyes were wet with tears of regret for his betrayal. He was aware that the one who calls is 'the Messiah, the Son of the living God'.[2] This later invitation came with the explicit promise of a path marked by suffering.[3] The words 'follow me' were identical each time, but the meaning different. His invitation is always to follow from somewhere, from where we are. The focus is always the same ('follow *me*'), but the implications

---

1 Matthew 4:19.
2 Matthew 16:16.
3 John 21:18–19.

differ and deepen as the journey progresses and the relationship develops.

To draw again on our rewilding metaphor, saying 'yes' to Jesus is to introduce into the environment of our lives a species so other and so powerful that total transformation is inevitable. C. S. Lewis had no doubt about the implications of introducing the one he referred to as 'the Great Interferer'. Like releasing a long-extinct species into an unenclosed landscape, Lewis tells of his realisation that, 'There was no region even in the innermost depth of one's soul (nay, there least of all) which one could surround with a barbed wire fence and guard with a notice No Admittance.'[4]

The New Testament's vision of Church is not a herd of people with common beliefs or shared behaviours. Rather, it is a community centred on Jesus, comprising people whose orientating of their lives upon Jesus draws them together in a shared quest of Christward transformation. Scholars of the Gospels point out that, beyond a decision to embrace the teaching of Jesus, the term 'disciple' is used to refer to people whose response led them on fundamentally different roads to each other. Nowhere is a line drawn between those who literally followed him as he travelled and the much wider group that Jesus himself counted as disciples. These included those who were 'outside the circle of those who had formally declared for him'[5] but who demonstrated by their actions their decision to embrace the Way Jesus taught and lived.[6] In contrast, where Jesus is not at the centre of a community or organisation, regardless of whether it says 'church' on the label, it is in reality something else. Where, as Alison Morgan suggests, 'We have set up private clubs for those whose leisure interest is religion',[7] only

---

4 Lewis, C. S., 1984, *Surprised by Joy: The Shape of My Early Life*, New York, NY: Harcourt Brace, pp. 171–2.

5 Dunn, J., 1992, *Jesus' Call to Discipleship*, Cambridge: Cambridge University Press, pp. 108–13; Astley, J., 2015, 'Forming disciples: some educational and biblical reflections', *Rural Theology*, 13(1), pp. 4–17.

6 For example, those mentioned in Matthew 25:40, 45 and Mark 3:35.

7 Morgan, A., 2004, *The Wild Gospel*, Oxford: Monarch, p. 189.

a reintroduction of the Great Interferer will create Church. As many environmentalists are waking up to the vital importance of reintroducing certain species, those of us who care for the health and very existence of the Church need to consider our own reintroductions.

When, in 1999, the Church of Scotland's General Assembly appointed a special commission to 'to re-examine in depth the primary purposes of the Church and the shape of the Church of Scotland as we enter into the next Millennium', a group was drawn together that represented the many facets of such a theologically diverse and geographically scattered Church. This group, tasked with delivering what became the prophetic and influential report *A Church Without Walls*, went through their own 'reintroductions programme' during the two years of praying, studying, discussing and consulting between the commissioning and delivery of the report. Meeting with several of them in 2019 to reflect on why the report failed to result in the transformation longed for by many within the denomination, it was fascinating and encouraging to witness the deep bonds of fellowship that had been forged by intentionally journeying with Jesus all those years earlier. Far from being a case of 'birds of a feather', these were women and men brought together precisely because of their differences, but who discovered that their desire for Jesus to be the centre and touchstone of their lives and of the Church was stronger than their many differences.

Discussion around some of the factors that thwarted the report's impact was sad to witness: ambiguous decision-making processes, the vested interests of powerful individuals, a lack of initiative regionally and locally in creating new ecclesial communities, the Church's failure to adequately reform its training and support for members, elders and ministers, the list goes on. But what I will always remember of that gathering was the spontaneous laughter, tinged with regret, triggered by the memory that, when it came to finalising the report, they had seriously considered presenting a two-word report, with all the rest of their reflections and suggestions appearing as footnotes. The two words would have been 'Follow me'. Although they eventually presented the report in a more conventional style, its core point is clear: '"Follow me". These two words of Jesus Christ offer us the purpose, shape and process of continuous reform of the Church ... The Church of Jesus Christ is about nothing more and nothing less than this.'[8] Nothing more. Nothing less. William Barclay, commenting on Saint Paul's own understanding of the Church's fundamental nature in his letter to the Ephesians, reminds us that 'Its unity comes not from organization, or ritual, or liturgy, or worship. Its unity comes from Christ.'[9] Or in the words of one who we often refer to as a 'Father of the Church', but who, in the context of this discussion we should perhaps identify as simply one of the early followers of Jesus, Saint Ignatius (AD 35–107/140), Bishop of Antioch: 'Where Christ is, there is the Church.'[10]

It was dark

There can be few scenes in the New Testament record more evocative of the contemporary Church in the Western world than the passage quoted from at the beginning of this chapter. A small clutch of devoted souls are straining at the oars. Far from land, pitched and tossed by the mounting waves, their boat feels insignificant and fragile. Jesus was nowhere to be seen. 'It was dark'.

The day had started with great excitement. Clustered around Jesus, they had eagerly reported all that had occurred as they had stepped out in modest faith. Following his directions they had anointed the sick and taught the people God had brought across their path. On a previous occasion Jesus had accompanied them, worked alongside them, but this time he had sent them out, two by two. It had been scary, but now there was so

8 The General Assembly of the Church of Scotland, 2001, *Church Without Walls*, www.churchofscotland.org.uk/__data/assets/pdf_file/0006/11787/CWW_REPORT_for_website_2Nov2012.pdf, p. 8.

9 Barclay, W., 2010, *The Letters to the Galatians and Ephesians*, Edinburgh: Saint Andrew Press, p. 119.

10 Ignatius of Antioch, 'ubi Christus, ibi ecclesia', *Letter to the Smyrnaeans*, p. 8.

much to report: so exciting, just as he said, so exhausting, no time to eat.

Jesus' response had been welcome balm to their compassion-fatigued minds and bodies: the suggestion of quiet, rest and time away – with him. But it was not to be. More crowds, more need, more giving out, wonderful things, Jesus doing the most amazing things, and misunderstandings too. Finally, realising their utter exhaustion, he had packed them off, got them away from there, into a boat, while he dismissed the crowds and found a place to pray.

Now weariness had turned to utter exhaustion. Struggling to make headway against the intensifying wind, Jesus, it seemed, was far away. Perhaps John's words express both the time of day and the prevailing mood: 'It was dark.'[11]

Then Jesus comes to them. Bruce Milne observes that 'the disciples are apparently more afraid of the saviour than they are of the storm',[12] but then their terror turns to joy. Once again they hear that phrase, that identification with the Almighty: 'I AM'.[13] He may have passed from their minds, but they had never been beyond his awareness. In their state of intense weariness he may have faded within their debilitated consciousness, but their struggles had not eluded his attention.[14]

The 'reintroduction' of Jesus is indispensable to the initiation of renewal. In fact, perhaps 'renewal' is too superficial a term for what occurs when any person or group is re-centred on Jesus. When Australian missiologists and church pioneers Mike Frost and Alan Hirsch call for a radical re-centring of the Church around the 'Wild Messiah' in their appropriately titled book, ReJesus, they argue that this constitutes a 'refounding': 'Rather than call this reformation, we will call this task refounding the church because it raises the issue of the church's true founder or foundation.'[15] Without a constantly

---

11 John 6:17 (NIV).
12 Milne, B., 1993, *The Message of John*, London: IVP, p. 108.
13 John 6:20 (NLT).
14 Mark 6:48.
15 Frost, M. and A. Hirsch, 2009, *ReJesus*, Peabody, MA: Hendrickson, p. 5.

refreshed consciousness of his presence, childlike curiosity and uncomplicated trust become overgrown by religious piety or a creeping sense of being in control.

Rewilding the Church is not a call to spend more hours on our knees, although for some it might mean that. Rather, it is a refocusing of our attention on Jesus, a reinstating of him at the heart of everything. The Victorian Baptist preacher Charles Spurgeon, who preached and wrote with great passion about prayer, is reputed to have rarely prayed for more than five minutes, but rarely let five minutes elapse without prayer.[16] For individual disciples and as groups of any form or size within his Church, refocusing on Jesus is the most imperative, transformative, life-giving, terrifying, hopeful, empowering enterprise possible. For the follower of Christ, the pathway to refresh or recover or restore vision, faith and vitality always begins here. The single essential essence of being disciples is that we seek, repeatedly and frequently, to re-centre our lives on him.

Discipleship, the act of *being* a disciple, sometimes understood as an educational endeavour or as a process of inducting less experienced believers into conformity of belief and tradition, is in fact intensely relational, continuous and all-encompassing. How could it be anything other than relational? While the teachings of Jesus provide the richest source of truth and wisdom, the one we follow is not an idea to be contemplated or a hypothesis to be proved. While his power to create and to restore is beyond imagining, he is not a force to invoke or harness. 'God reveals himself in personal relationship and only in personal relationship ... There is nothing in or of God that is impersonal, nothing abstract ...'[17] It is in the context of this relationship and as we nurture that relationship that, gradually but resolutely, often imperceptibly but occasionally dramatically, a Christ-ward transformation occurs. It is

---

16 Michael, L., 2010, *Spurgeon on Leadership: Key Insights for Christian Leaders from the Prince of Preachers*, Grand Rapids, MI: Kregel, p. 70.

17 Peterson, E., 2013, *Practice Resurrection: A Conversation on Growing Up in Christ*, Grand Rapids, MI: Eerdmans, pp. 86–7.

a life-long undertaking and a daily discipline. It is a whole-of-life reorientation of life. It is an all-embracing, all-inclusive, all-pervading process of rehabilitation.

Ripping up the fences

In summer 2019, the decision of Bristol Zoological Society's Wild Place Project to enable 'Bears and wolves to coexist in UK woods for first time in 1,000 years'[18] grabbed some headline space and sparked some keen debate about the wisdom of reintroducing these kinds of long-absent species as part of efforts to rewild ancient woodlands. The reality turned out to be less dramatic than the headlines. European brown bears, thought to have become extinct in the British wilds in medieval times, and grey wolves – which roamed free until the seventeenth century – along with lynxes and wolverines, 'coexist' in a space known as Bear Wood near Bristol, an enclosed area of ancient woodland the size of about six football pitches. At the time of writing, although the intention is for them to share a single enclosure, these four species are still separated from one another by other internal fencing. As zoo enclosures go, 'Bear Wood' is extremely generous, but compared to the natural habitats of these creatures it is minuscule; as an example of rewilding, it is nothing of the sort. Rewilding involves removing fences. One of the best known rewilding projects in the UK is the Knepp Estate in West Sussex. This once intensively farmed 3,500-acre estate, about which we shall hear more in later chapters, began its journey into rewilding in 2001 with the removal of 70 miles of fencing. Those who want to allow some rewilding within their own gardens are advised to make holes in any fencing, ensuring that the comings and goings of small animals are not impeded by the human desire for privacy.

---

18 Morris, S., 2019, 'Bears and wolves to coexist in UK woods for first time in 1,000 years', 16 July, *The Guardian*, www.theguardian.com/uk-news/2019/jul/16/bears-and-wolves-to-coexist-in-uk-woods-in-conservation-project (accessed 18.07.2019).

Rewilding and fences do not go well together. One of the great challenges for the Church is that Jesus, our wild Messiah, in his example and teaching, while not blatantly anti-institutional, *is* consistently subversive. The world Jesus knew was criss-crossed by powerful, even if often invisible, barriers: religious, ethnic and gender barriers for starters, and throughout the Gospels we find Jesus treating these fences with indifference. As the Dutch theologian Abraham Kuyper stated, 'there is not a square inch of the universe over which Jesus Christ does not exclaim "Mine!"'.[19] Or in the words of Jesus himself, 'All authority in heaven and on earth has been given to me.'[20] There can be no fencing off, nothing is ring-fenced from the influence of Jesus. Which is why, as Frost and Hirsch remind us, 'we must constantly return to Jesus to authenticate as well as legitimize ourselves as his people. We have no other Archimedean point ...'[21] Again and again we need to invite him to have free rein in our lives and in those manifestations of Church we connect with.

Following Jesus and creating institutions do not fit easily together. Having spent a lot of time over several years listening to and surveying hundreds of Christians who are not engaged with a local church congregation, perhaps the most consistent theme to emerge is a frustration with institutional ways of following Jesus. A clear majority of those so-called 'church-less Christians' surveyed agreed with the statement 'I feel part of the worldwide Christian community'. Most have local or virtual connections of informal fellowship, but the structures and policies of church networks and denominations are often described as hampering rather than enhancing their following, hindering rather than fostering faith. The understanding and experience of Church that such people seem to be developing over time is of a community of disciples, joined together in all

---

19 Quote from Kuyper's inaugural address at the dedication of the Free University. Found in Bratt, J. (ed.), 1998, *Abraham Kuyper: A Centennial Reader*, Grand Rapids, MI: Eerdmans, p. 488.

20 Matthew 28:18.

21 Frost, M. and A. Hirsch, 2009, *ReJesus*, Peabody, MA: Hendrickson, p. 8.

kinds of diverse ways, ranging from the formal structures of denominations to casual friendships (face to face and virtual), networks of mutual encouragement and partnerships focused on specific purposes.

People who have disengaged from local congregational life often do so after a lengthy period of deep commitment and are forced to engage in reflection about the nature of the Church. What seems to be emerging from that is a reminder of two twin truths. First, as per the historic creeds, the Church is one. And second, that singular Church is expressed in the most astonishing and continuously changing diversity. While following Jesus draws us into a relationship of growing constancy as we learn to heed his instruction to 'remain in me',[22] the communities that emerge from doing that together will always be in flux; in Küng's words, '... essentially an interim Church, a Church in transition'.[23] The elemental oneness of the Church should drive us towards *being* one in reality, while at the same time embracing and celebrating the huge diversity of expressions, the visible elements of which will always be the tip of the proverbial iceberg. Not only does the New Testament 'not even suggest that the diversity of local churches poses a threat to, or is inconsistent with, the unity of the church',[24] it is clear that even in those earliest of times, unity and diversity were two of the most striking hallmarks of the Jesus movement. In his thorough academic study of the early Church, Professor James Dunn expresses amazement at how such a diversity of expression could be manifestations of the same 'one Church' and concludes that it is 'the unity of the faith in Jesus the man now exalted' and 'the unity of love for fellow believers'[25] that bound this dynamic and multi-faceted movement as one. In every generation since, despite splits and schisms, these same forces, both elements of the same Spirit's power at work, have

22 John 15:4–8.
23 Küng, H., 1967, *The Church*, London: Burns and Oates, p. 131.
24 McGrath, A. E., 2017, *Theology: The Basics*, Hoboken, NJ: Wiley-Blackwell, p. 153.
25 Dunn, J., 1977, *Unity and Diversity in the New Testament: An Inquiry into the Character of Earliest Christianity*, Philadelphia, PA: Westminster, p. 378.

continued to create the one Church, sometimes visible, often not, straddling the globe and spanning the ages.

Reintroducing the keystone species

When advocates of rewilding promote the reintroduction of certain 'keystone species', it is not just about adding one more species to the list of an area's wildlife. A keystone species is an organism whose presence or absence has a *disproportionate* effect on other organisms in the system. Whether animal, plant or fungi, they have a critical role in the health and maintenance of the ecosystem. Where they have been absent, their reintroduction triggers transformation and kickstarts reinvigoration.

While we have been aware for a long time that changes in one level in the food chain have impacts on subsequent levels, it is now clear that the depth and breadth of those influences can be out of all proportion to the scale of the original change. In recent years our understanding of what have been called 'trophic cascades' has grown enormously. These are powerful indirect interactions that can control entire ecosystems. They might be 'top-down' cascades, where decline or increase in certain top level predators lead to deep and extensive impacts throughout the whole system. Equally, changes at a primary level, such as in plankton population, can cause 'bottom-up trophic cascades', triggering multiple domino effects throughout the environment.

Perhaps the most frequently cited example of trophic cascades is the return of the grey wolf to the Yellowstone National Park in the western United States. Having been absent from the region since the 1920s, a small population of wolves was reintroduced in the mid-1990s. The extent of the impacts has been remarkable. For seventy years the elk population had been free to graze unimpeded. Following the reintroduction, not only was the elk population diminished, but their behaviour also changed. The threat of predation by wolves led to changes in the elk's feeding habits. Species of plant and tree that had previously been heavily browsed began to thrive for the first time in decades. Changes in the course of rivers, an increase in the beaver population and adaptations to soil composition are among the numerous knock-on effects from the return of that single species.[26]

Proponents of rewilding point out that, while human management of the environment has tended to result in vicious circles of diminishing biodiversity and a tendency towards monoculture, the reintroduction of keystone species triggers trophic cascades that conspire to form virtuous spirals of increased diversity and complexity; reintroductions of native species can catalyse reinvigoration of one aspect of the biosphere and these trigger and foster regeneration in other spheres. Keystone species not only play a crucial role in maintaining the health and appropriate population levels of other organisms, their presence also modifies the behaviour of other species. In due course, species that were previously inhibited begin to thrive; others that had been dominant are forced to change their habits.

How might our understanding of the transformational impact of 'keystone species' inspire a renewed relationship with the ultimate 'keystone', the 'chief cornerstone',[27] Jesus? At first glance, the organic, dynamic influence of keystone species grates with the cold, inanimate, solidness of the architectural metaphor of 'the cornerstone'. However, the journey of that stone through the prophets into the Gospels and through the epistles leads towards a living, breathing community in which we are all joined securely to Jesus and to one another. In Isaiah's prophecies we catch glimpses of a rock that offers 'the only foundation of hope ... laid in Zion, in the eternal counsels of God';[28] it is a stone that is carefully 'tried' and chosen, 'a precious cornerstone'.[29] In the collection of psalms

---

26 Ripple, W. J. and R. L. Beschta, 2012, 'Trophic cascades in Yellowstone: The first 15 years after wolf reintroduction', *Biological Conservation*, 145, pp. 205–13.

27 Different translations favour 'keystone' and 'cornerstone', but the meaning is similar, whichever is preferred.

28 Henry, M., 2003, *Concise Commentary on the Whole Bible*, Chicago, IL: Moody, p. 526.

29 Isaiah 28:16.

known as the *Hallal* (associated with *hallelujah*),[30] a collection of hymns of praise used during Passover, a vision of coming salvation is expressed as a stone that the builders dismiss as useless, but which turns out to be the most crucial of all,[31] the keystone. It seems likely that it was during the Passover week of his own crucifixion that Jesus referred to that prophetic passage as being fulfilled in himself.[32] Knowing the importance of the keystone imagery to his hearers, Peter chose to use it in his challenge to religious leaders following Pentecost.[33] Then, later, he adopted the keystone metaphor again in his letters, but struggling with the limitations of a construction metaphor for what is an organic and relational reality he adopted the phrase 'living stone': Jesus, the keystone, is a living stone and we too are urged to offer ourselves as living stones that can be used 'for the construction of a sanctuary vibrant with life';[34] as we welcome the keystone to involve us as living stones, we will be 'built into a house for worship';[35] for a building extension to be strong, new stones need to be 'tied into' the existing stones so that all are interconnected and, crucially, 'toed into' the keystone.

When Paul celebrated the extraordinary way in which God has reconciled people to himself and each other through Jesus, he explained the new position in which they found themselves using three powerful metaphors: a kingdom, a family and the temple.[36] In terms of kingdom, those 'in Christ' are transformed from being foreigners to being citizens. In the second metaphor, we are no longer outsiders, but family members. Third, the metaphor of a temple draws attention to two essen-

---

30 Psalms 113—118; see Brueggemann, W. and W. Bellinger, 2014, *Psalms*, Cambridge: Cambridge University Press, p. 507.

31 Psalm 118:22.

32 All the synoptic Gospels record this (see Matthew 21:42; Mark 12:10; Luke 20:17) and although they do not appear to represent a chronological account throughout, it does appear likely that this teaching took place in that final holy week.

33 Acts 4:11.

34 1 Peter 2:5 (MSG).

35 1 Peter 2:5 (NIrV®).

36 Ephesians 2:19–22.

tial elements: 'the foundation of the apostles and prophets' and 'Christ Jesus himself, the chief cornerstone'.

For Paul, the cornerstone is essential for both the unity and the growth of the Church; the two are inextricably intertwined – in fact, totally interdependent. 'The unity and the growth of the church are coupled, and Jesus Christ is the secret of both … Christ the cornerstone is indispensable to the church's unity and growth.'[37] And of course the figurative use of building terminology can go a step further when that building is the temple. The great Jerusalem temple, whether that built by Solomon, Zerubbabel or Herod, was understood as being 'the dwelling place of God', exactly the claim Paul makes for the Church: 'In him the whole structure is joined together and grows into a holy temple in the Lord; in whom you also are built together spiritually into a dwelling place for God.'[38]

Of course the usefulness of any metaphor extends only so far. For example, there are many keystone species, but only one Cornerstone. Whereas calls for the reintroduction of these species are usually in situations where those species have been destroyed through persecution or habitat destruction, nobody is suggesting that Christ is ever entirely absent from the lives of individual believers or wherever two or three gather in his name. However, if Christ the cornerstone is the source of unity and growth, when those characteristics are lacking it makes sense to question whether there is a need for some kind of 'reintroducing'. In the natural environment reintroductions usually become necessary because certain keystone species have been squeezed out by human activity. They are then reintroduced by our intervention. In the Church too, where we have lived and worked and planned and managed in ways that have crowded out Jesus himself, we can also be the ones to initiate a reintroduction.

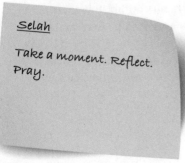

Selah

Take a moment. Reflect. Pray.

---

37 Stott, J., 1991, *The Message of Ephesians*, London: IVP, p. 109.
38 Ephesians 2:21–22.

Following the invisible man

It's tricky to follow someone we cannot see, but, individually and together, we can learn to do that once more.

Just north of Inverness is a peninsula of rich agricultural land and forestry, the Black Isle, pointing out into the North Sea. From its south shore, thrusting out into the Moray Firth is another peninsula, almost a microcosm of the Black Isle itself. With a fine sandy beach on each side, the narrow finger of Chanonry Ness provides a fine circular walk out to the squat lighthouse crouching at its seaward end and back to one of the villages of Fortrose or Rosemarkie. In common with most lighthouses, the one at Chanonry Point inhabits an exposed spot and, especially when the tide is turning, the surrounding waters are often whipped up into foaming whirls and waves as a powerful tidal race is forced through the narrow neck of water separating the Outer Firth from the Firth of Inverness.

Approaching Chanonry Point on a squally September day, I was surprised to see a small crowd of more than a dozen hardy souls, not walking with any sense of purpose, but apparently staring out to sea. Drawing closer it became clear that these people were in no hurry. Some had brought camping chairs. Hot drinks were being poured from flasks, but no one's gaze dropped from the froth and surge of the surrounding sea. A fine display of optical technology was on display: binoculars and cameras. There was a hum of cheery chat and laughter, but all eyes were firmly fixed on the briny turbulence in front of them. And then I remembered. Local newspapers had reported the frustrations of local people at the increasing frequency of chaotic congestion at the small parking area as swarms of nature lovers were being drawn to the Point by promises of bottlenose dolphins, brought close to shore in their search for prey. Here were people, drawn together by a shared hope, utterly focused, the embodiment of expectancy. A sighting of these exquisite creatures is far from guaranteed, but it is possible. Certainly those people were infinitely more likely to see the object of their optimism than most people in the UK. Their hope had brought them to a 'thin place', where the record of sightings is unusually high; their attitude of expectation meant that if so much as the tip of a dorsal fin broke the surface, they were ready.

The absolute attention and dogged perseverance of the dolphin watchers spoke to me of the call to abide or remain mentioned above. In his delightful booklet *Being Disciples*, Rowan Williams sees a disciple's call to constancy as a reflection of the relationship between Jesus and his Father: 'The relationship of Jesus to the Father is ... sustained, eternal and unbroken.'[39] And of course, his side of the relationship *is* constant: 'For I am convinced that neither death, nor life, nor angels, nor rulers, nor things present, nor things to come, nor powers, nor height, nor depth, nor anything else in all creation, will be able to separate us from the love of God in Christ Jesus our Lord.'[40] The challenge is for us to grow in loyalty and fidelity in this relationship. Being a disciple involves choosing to be aware of that love and to nurture an awareness of his presence. Like the dolphin watchers we take ourselves to those places where, throughout history, we know that the invisible man has been sighted. I'm not referring particularly to the geographical places that have been historically important, places of pilgrimage, 'thin places' where the distance between heaven and earth seems to be unusually small and 'the walls are weak', although these may be important to those who are privileged to visit them. I'm thinking more of *our* sites and occasions of prayer, study, fellowship, contemplation, wherever they are.

Just as the dolphin viewers orientate themselves seawards and scan the waves, we too learn attitudes of attention and expectancy. Like nature watchers of all kinds, and along with our sisters and brothers who have walked in this Jesus way before us, we realise the value of quiet and solitude and other factors that stack the odds of encounter. Also in common with those who spend long hours in the hope of a glimpse of a wonder of nature, we find that the call to constancy is an invitation to spend many an hour in the presence of our extraordinary God that feels remarkably unremarkable, long

39 Williams, R., 2016, *Being Disciples: Essentials of the Christian Life*, London: SPCK, p. 14.
40 Romans 8:38–39.

periods of steady faithfulness punctuated with only the occasional flash of the kind of encounter that stands out from the ordinary. The hundreds of hours I have spent walking along the River Spey blur together into a homogenous memory, but I will never forget the only two occasions in thirty years when I witnessed the flash of a kingfisher's wings, nor the time when, as I poured out my heart to God regarding a personal tragedy, I was blessed with a glorious double rainbow.

Like Jacob when he awoke after a dream so powerful that he was forced to conclude 'Surely the Lord is in this place – and I did not know it!'[41] we are sometimes taken by surprise, ready or not. And yet there is no doubting the importance of cultivating habits of steady faithfulness that enable a patient heavenward orientation and expectancy. Philip Yancey, wrestling with the challenges of *Reaching Out for the Invisible God*, notes that he seldom runs into clues of God's presence 'unless I am looking'.[42] Our conscious turning Godwards, our sincere seeking, makes thick places thinner. Hence what seem to be rash promises on God's part, from Jeremiah to Jesus: 'You will seek me and find me when you seek me with all your heart[43] ... everyone who asks receives, and everyone who searches finds, and for everyone who knocks, the door will be opened.'[44]

Following together

The priority being given in several church denominations to a renewed focus on understanding what it means to be disciples and how we can best be encouraged and equipped for that lifelong journey in the contemporary world, is heart-warming. The Church of England's *Developing Discipleship* report in 2015[45]

41 Genesis 28:16.

42 Yancey, P., 2000, *Reaching Out for the Invisible God*, Grand Rapids, MI: Zondervan, p. 89.

43 Jeremiah 29:13.

44 Matthew 7:8.

45 Archbishops' Council, 2015, *Developing Discipleship*. GS 1977, www.churchofengland.org/media-centre/developing-discipleship-report-2015.aspx (accessed 01.12.2019).

marked the beginning of 'a conversation about Christian discipleship' based on an understanding of Church being 'called to be and to become a community of missionary disciples'.[46] In 2019 the Church of Scotland's General Assembly identified 'the creation and deepening of a culture of discipleship' as a top priority.[47] This kind of fresh awareness of the need for individuals to grow in faith is timely. My own research in Scotland confirmed the findings of others in New Zealand and England and Wales in finding that many Christians who used to be involved with a local church report a key reason for their disengagement as failing to find within congregational life helpful contexts in which to explore questions and doubts and apply Jesus' teaching to everyday life.[48]

In promoting a rewilding of the Church and a reintroducing of the Great Interferer it is not intended to suggest that Jesus has been wilfully excluded or deliberately neglected. However, the fact is that without repeated, deliberate refocusing on Christ, our individual intentions and our corporate efforts to recalibrate life with him and his character are quickly diverted. When the writer to the Hebrews exhorted his readers 'Let us keep our eyes fixed on Jesus, on whom our faith depends from beginning to end'[49] there was no implication that they had never done so. Rather, there was an acknowledgement of what we know from our own lived experience: that, while we have resolved to centre our lives on Christ, maintaining the simple trust and eager seeking that characterises a healthy faith is an ongoing battle. We never outgrow the need to refocus on our Saviour. Without it, self seizes control and Jesus becomes a pastime, 'Lord' in name only. In the words of Eugene Peterson,

---

46 Archbishops' Council, *Developing Discipleship*.

47 *Report of the Mission and Discipleship Council*, Deliverance 2: https://ga.churchofscotland.org.uk/storage/uploads/mission-and-disci pleship-council.pdf (accessed 01.12.2019).

48 Aisthorpe, S., 2016, *The Invisible Church: Learning from the Experiences of Churchless Christians*, Edinburgh, Saint Andrew Press, chapter 4, 'Exit Routes', pp. 57–77.

49 Hebrews 12:2 (GNT).

'Humility recedes as competence increases'[50] or, worse still, 'instead of living as we started out – child followers of Jesus – we become bosses on behalf of Jesus'.[51] We see this creeping tendency in our own lives and find its corporate manifestations in our groups, congregations and networks.

Introducing and reintroducing the Great Interferer is the essence of the Christian life for each of us, but also for our groups, gatherings and institutions. They too need to be continually reJesused. One idea, so obvious, so effective and yet often neglected, is an approach advanced in the *Church Without Walls* report mentioned above. Congregations or groups are encouraged 'to choose to study, reflect on and live by one Gospel for one year'. Crucially, those with the courage to embark on such a journey were urged to 'let Jesus shape the life and structure of the congregation'.[52] This is not the place for prescribing any particular methods of engaging with Scripture together. Every tradition has developed its own treasure trove of approaches and resources. Explore the riches developed in other cultures and eras and do not neglect what is close to home. More important than the method is the attitude.

Like any reintroduction programme, key to a genuinely transformative impact is the environment into which the Great Interferer is released. Is it a habitat in which the potential impact of the one introduced will be realised? Asking how the ongoing interaction with a Gospel challenges a group or organisation is one thing, but having the courage and commitment to respond to what is discerned is what will lead to actual change. To turn to a different metaphor for a moment, the seed can be planted, but the fruit depends to a significant extent on the nature of the soil. There is openness in really first-rate soil. Pockets of air and moisture feed roots and encourage them

---

50 Peterson, E., 2013, *Practice Resurrection: A Conversation on Growing Up in Christ*, Grand Rapids, MI: Eerdmans, p. 191.

51 Peterson, *Practice Resurrection*, p. 192.

52 The General Assembly of the Church of Scotland, 2001, *Church Without Walls*, www.churchofscotland.org.uk/__data/assets/pdf_file/00 06/11787/CWW_REPORT_for_website_2Nov2012.pdf, p. 3 (accessed 27.11.2019).

deeper. So it is with the impact of a corporate journey with Jesus through Matthew, Mark, Luke or John; an attitude of honest reflection and genuine willingness for change is a prerequisite for a bumper crop. The colloquial assertion 'honest to God' is rarely used as a genuine reminder of consciously standing in an attitude of transparency before one's Creator, but it actually expresses well the stance required in realigning our lives with Christ, whether individually or together. We need to come in plain, unpretentious sincerity and invite Jesus to cast his holy and loving gaze over our lives and organisations.

Having accompanied congregations through journeys of refounding over extended periods, I know that there are no short cuts to creating a culture of Christ-centred openness and courageous response. Good soil is the legacy of careful cultivation. Promoting an attitude of mutual respect, a commitment to deep listening and a recognising of every other disciple as a unique and precious gift is the equivalent of introducing rich organic matter into the seed bed. These are the qualities of fertile habitats, communities primed for encounter and refounding.

As we seek and respond, more insight is revealed, more is discovered, and more is required. What Thomas Merton observed in the personal walk of faith is true as we seek the way together: 'We receive enlightenment only in proportion as we give ourselves more and more completely to God by humble submission and love.'[53] This is rewilding; the journey unfolding with each step; an authentic adventure.

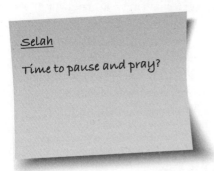

Selah

Time to pause and pray?

53 Merton, T., 1955, *No Man is an Island*, New York, NY: Harcourt, Brace & Co., p. 241.

5

LISTEN: Tuning In and Joining In

'My sheep listen to my voice;
I know them, and they follow me.'
John 10:27 (NIV)

STOP, look and listen

By the late 1990s the owners and workers of Knepp Estate in West Sussex had been persevering for a very long time. Like many farmers working in situations that might be called 'marginal', turning a profit had proved extremely difficult for a long time and some years proved to be impossible. The owner, Charlie Burrell, had been 'doing what every modern farmer is supposed to do: rationalise, intensify, diversify and, if possible, spread the fixed costs over a larger area'.[1] Trying to compete with larger, industrialised farms on better soils constantly whittled down morale. There were occasional signs of encouragement, when the extreme effort, careful planning and the use of modern technology yielded a slight surplus. However, as Charlie's wife Isabella records, 'Ultimately it was farming itself that undermined us. After fifteen years we had made a surplus in only two.'[2] Few of us can imagine the burden of responsibility and the weight of expectation experienced by someone who inherits a 3,500-acre estate that has been in the family for 220 years. The pressure to 'keep things going' and, not least, to preserve the livelihoods of faithful and hardworking employees must be immense.

---

1 Tree, I., 2018, *Wilding: The Return of Nature to a British Farm*, London: Picador, p. 32.
2 Tree, *Wilding*, p. 36.

By the end of the 1990s those involved in the management
of the Knepp Estate had a growing sense that their farming
practices were at odds with the environment. The soil could no
longer sustain ever more intensive agriculture. The soil itself,
a heavy clay over a bedrock of limestone, 'persistently threw
a spanner in the works'.[3] Eventually the realisation dawned
that they could no longer work against the environment. The
soil itself was rebelling and the estate's debts were mounting.
In February 2000, the heartbreaking decision was made to sell
the dairy herds and farm machinery, to put the arable farming
out to contract, and to take a drastically different direction.

Around this time Charlie came under the influence of two
ideas he had never previously encountered. First, a consultant
visiting the estate to advise regarding a particularly ancient
oak tree opened his eyes to the vast timescales over which
the processes of nature shape our landscapes. An oak tree,
left to its own devices, 'grows for 300 years, rests for another
300 years and spends the last 300 gracefully declining',
Charlie was informed. The second insight that revolutionised
Charlie's thinking came from an obscure Dutch publication
translated into English making its way into his hands. From
reading *Grazing Ecology and Forest History* by ground-
breaking ecologist Dr Frans Vera, Charlie began to realise that
introducing some hardy breeds of grazing animals (long horn
cattle, Tamworth pigs, Exmoor ponies and indigenous deer)
as proxies for some long-absent species could create forces of
'natural disturbance' and help the landscape to recover.

Beginning with an ancient park at the heart of the estate,
Knepp became the focus of a project the owners describe in
terms of 'allowing nature to take the driving seat'. They realised
that they had been 'working against the land', rather than with
it. No goals were set. Instead, natural processes were permitted
and encouraged. The ground that had long been constrained
by intensive agriculture was opened up and disturbed by the
rootling and browsing of the free-ranging pigs and cattle.
An easing of the land began and processes of recovery were

---

3 Tree, *Wilding*, p. 34.

initiated. By 2002, substantive change was already obvious. 'Most conspicuous of all was the ambient noise: the low-level surround-sound thrumming of insects – something we hadn't even known we'd been missing.'[4] Even that early in the project, the owner describes walking through knee-deep wild flowers and disturbing clouds of butterflies. It took years for the rewilding ideas at Knepp to be recognised, but in 2010 Professor Sir John Lawton, author of the 2010 *Making Space for Nature* report, described it as 'one of the most exciting wildlife conservation projects in the UK, and indeed in Europe ... it fills me with hope'.[5]

Sometimes our vision calls us to perseverance; sometimes it requires us to abandon conventional wisdom and embark on a radically different path. History will celebrate the fact that the owners and managers of Knepp Estate listened to what the soil was saying. No doubt they will be seen as pioneers and people who recognised the early signs of something that others will see later, as those signs become more blatant and more difficult to reverse. According to the United Nations Food and Agriculture Organization (FAO) report in 2015, about a third of the planet's soil is moderately to highly degraded due to processes such as compaction, erosion, acidification and pollution. In the UK the cost of our degrading soils is estimated at between £900 million and £1.4 billion each year.[6] 'The Nation that destroys its soil destroys itself'.[7]

When we realise that something major is wrong, it takes great courage to stop. Mostly we do more and work harder, knuckle down and intensify, but sometimes it is time to stop. A role model in the Scriptures is Nehemiah. We tend to think of him as a man of action. His legacy was an incredible building project, completed in record time and against stern

---

4 Tree, *Wilding*, p. 44.

5 www.knepp.co.uk/background.

6 Tree, *Wilding*, p. 275.

7 Letter from US President Franklin D. Roosevelt, to all State Governors, on a Uniform Soil Conservation Law, 26 February 1937. www.oxfordreference.com/view/10.1093/acref/9780191843730.001.0001/q-oro-ed5-00008907 (accessed 14.10.2019).

opposition. And yet, when he was first confronted with news of the catastrophic situation faced by his sisters and brothers in Jerusalem we are told that his first reaction was to 'sit down'.[8] He stopped. He allowed the impact of the devastating news of his own people's hardship and suffering to wash over him and he wept. Instead of rushing to respond, rather than allowing his passion to dictate his actions, he then took time to listen and discern: 'fasting and praying before the God of heaven'[9] and, later, a thorough assessment of the challenge at hand.[10] Rewilding the Church is not about implementing our best ideas with unusual passion; it requires stopping or slowing down, a conscious setting aside of preconceptions and a determination to discern what God is doing and our role in that.

The dawning

The courageous American biologist Rachel Carson, whose book *Silent Spring* was one of the earliest warnings of the disastrous consequences of synthetic pesticides on the planet's ecosystems, said that when we listen to that astonishing symphony of birdsong we call the dawn chorus, 'one hears the throb of life itself'.[11]

Have you ever listened to the dawn chorus? I don't mean have you ever *heard* it. Have you actually *listened* to the dawn chorus? Many of us will have noticed it when we have been forced to leave home earlier than usual. Or perhaps we have been annoyed by it when sultry weather conditions have forced us to sleep with the bedroom windows open. Although it is available, free of cost, across the country, for much of the year, I suspect that few people get around to actually listening to this inconspicuous wonder of nature.

---

8 Nehemiah 1:4.
9 Nehemiah 1:4.
10 Nehemiah 2:11–16.
11 Carson, R., 1965, *The Sense of Wonder*, New York, NY: Harper-Collins, p. 69.

May and June are the peak time for this avian extravaganza. The first birds begin to sing about an hour before sunrise and, as different species add their voices to the swelling choir, the chorus reaches a magnificent crescendo in the periods just before and after sunrise. Come the spring and summer months, if you can bear to set the alarm sufficiently early, it may do you the world of good. Psychologists report that there is strong evidence for the therapeutic benefits of birdsong. Bird sounds feature commonly in studies that explore attention restoration and stress recovery via natural sounds and soundscapes.[12]

For those with ears to hear, the dawn chorus is full of meaning and significance. Many of the voices of the birds are speaking about territory. Some are staking a claim to sources of food and others may be trying to attract a mate. If you listen carefully you'll notice that there is a regular sequence, with some species always starting before others. Among the earliest to rise are skylarks, hence the saying 'up with the lark'. Song thrushes, robins and blackbirds follow. These are the worm eaters, hence the proverb 'the early bird catches the worm'. It seems that, while most of us no longer even hear the dawn chorus, our ancestors not only heard it, they listened to it and they understood it.

Which makes one wonder, what else do we miss? Most of us live within earshot of dramatic displays of birdsong for substantial parts of the year, but rarely even register its occurrence.

When American author Annie Dillard was asked to write a paragraph for *Life* magazine on, of all things, 'the meaning of life', she suggested that: 'We are here to abet creation and to witness it, to notice each thing so each thing gets noticed ... so that creation need not play to an empty house.'[13] For those of us who seek to follow Christ, the creation speaks of the Creator. And for those 'with ears to hear', eyes to see, and

---

12 For example, Alvarsson, J. J., S. Wien, and M. E. Nilsson, 2010, 'Stress recovery during exposure to nature sound and environmental noise', *International Journal of Environmental Research and Public Health*, 7, pp. 1036–46.

13 Quoted in Gallagher, S. (ed.), 2005, *Where Faith Meets Culture: A Radix Magazine Anthology*, Eugene, OR: Cascade Books, p. 130.

other senses receptive to how our Lord might be communicating with us, the wonders of nature are one of the myriad ways in which we can perceive his guidance.

And yet in asking above 'what else do we miss?' I certainly do not mean to imply that unless we are constantly and deliberately listening for God then, for every moment we fail to be intentionally attuned to that still small voice, we are 'missing out' on guidance and blessing that can never be repeated. That way madness lies. Such an idea runs counter to the character of the God we know to be 'full of grace' and has more in common with contemporary culture's obsessive 'Fear of Missing Out' (FOMO).[14] Better than being motivated by a fearful FOMO is approaching the task of listening with a sense of holy privilege and profound pleasure.

From the psalms of King David, to James's letter to 'the tribes scattered abroad' and throughout the witness of saints and sages through the ages, there is unanimous assurance: 'The LORD is near to all who call on him',[15] 'Draw near to God, and he will draw near to you'.[16] Whereas today's dawn chorus has been and gone, never to be repeated, our gracious God eagerly awaits our attentive ear. And not just our ear, our curious gaze too, for 'listening' in terms of perceiving what God is revealing engages *all* the senses, as well as sanctified common sense, consecrated intuition, imagination and spiritual intelligence.

Celtic christianity

---

14 FOMO is a kind of social anxiety, a modern take on 'keeping up with the Joneses' in which social media fuels a fear that 'others might be having rewarding experiences from which one is absent' – leading to 'a desire to stay continually connected with what others are doing'. Przybylski, A. K. and colleagues (July 2013), 'Motivational, emotional, and behavioral correlates of fear of missing out', *Computers in Human Behavior*, 29(4), pp. 1841–8.

15 Psalm 145:18.

16 James 4:8.

Listening to God

The boggy path led steeply through pines, birches and heather. Squelching onwards, head down, hood up, I began a kind of prayer conversation. I had been asked to lead a workshop at a forthcoming summer school for people pioneering fresh expressions of Church and the title I'd been given was 'Listening to God'. My first thought had been 'Why me?'; I felt hopelessly unqualified for such a task. Knowing that, for me, the times when prayer flows most freely and when I most easily get ideas and insights are invariably in the Great Outdoors, it seemed that any further questions might best be asked on a walk.

The trail had been churned up by mountain bikers, the inside of my hood smelled of damp and dog biscuits; it hardly seemed the most conducive environment for a moment of intimacy with the Creator. But I began what I hoped might develop into some sort of conversation through some silent phrases. 'Here I am, Lord'. 'What about this "Listening to God" workshop?' An incident from some twenty years previous popped into my mind. I was sitting on a hillside above a village in Nepal. I asked God to intervene in what seemed to me to be a vicious circle of dire poverty and to bring liberation from a culture I understood to include a fear of evil spirits and a tendency towards fatalism. They were general prayers. While I believed that my requests were well within the powers of the Almighty, I was not expecting any immediate response. In fact, it felt as much a kind of catharsis as intercession. As I sat there, the scent of smouldering juniper wafted up from the village as households performed their morning *puja* (worship) rituals. The hollow clanging of bells and the shouts of herders echoed around the valley as a yak train lugged freight across the bridge below. I was enjoying simply being there, but then I became conscious of some words forming in my mind. 'What are *you* going to do about it?' I wasn't expecting that! No audible voice, but words that took me by surprise and would not go away ... words that became the foundation of other words in the months that followed ... words that shaped the way I understood some of the Scriptures I read. Those words became the basis of conversations with trusted friends and, in time, they are words that I realise in retrospect led me from one season of life into another radically different one, as, step by step, I followed what I became convinced was God's guiding.

Back on my boggy walk, the inside of my hood still smelling of damp and dog biscuits, I recognised that in all kinds of non-auditory-but-discernible-all-the-same ways I have heard God. That a simple Godward request on a Nepali hillside, and daring to contemplate that what had followed was part of a divine response, had led to one of my life's major crossroads, taking me from a life that I loved in Scotland into an unknown future in Nepal. As I stooped forward to see where best to put my boots to avoid sinking up to my ankles or slipping on to my backside, the rain or hail or whatever it was battered a little heavier on my head and shoulders. 'That was twenty years ago, Lord. How do you speak to me now? *Do* you speak to me now?' The previous weeks had been discouraging. I had sometimes questioned whether I was doing the right thing with my life. To be honest, God had seemed absent. Knowing that 'desert times' or 'wilderness experiences' are normal phases in the Christian journey doesn't make them any easier – especially when you need to deliver a workshop on 'Listening to God'! 'Where are you, God?' The same question I remember asking as a teenager, reading the Gideons Bible I'd been given at school, and asking sincerely, 'If you are there, God, please show me somehow.'

The rain had definitely turned to hail now and white balls began to collect around the edges of boggy puddles. I paused. For the first time since leaving the car park, I lifted my eyes from the metre or two of swampy path in front of me, pushed back my hood, and looked into the woodland around me. Suspended from stalks of heather and from the twigs and branches of birch trees were hundreds of cobwebs. Previously invisible, these tiny trampolines, each an intricate marvel of arachnid engineering, had been rendered visible by a quick shower of 'groupel'. These delicate hail-like pellets, formed from snow crystals in very particular meteorological conditions, were cradled in each web like eggs in a nest. In that moment my senses prickled with an appreciation of God's presence. Doubt was replaced by gratitude and some ideas for creating an opportunity for others to consider how we listen to God began to spark.

A few weeks later about thirty people gathered at the summer school for people interested in pioneering fresh expressions of Church to discuss how we listen to God. Most identified themselves as people who were not in the habit of listening to God. However, on further consideration, every person recognised that God had guided them, encouraged them, rebuked, taught, and many other things. One person in the group had once experienced God as an audible voice. The most common ways that participants had experienced God 'speaking' to them were through Scripture, through the words of other people and through circumstances. What became clear on that day and through a series of retreats in different parts of Scotland that followed is that God tends to speak to us in our 'mother tongue'. Unsurprisingly, the one who has known us since before our conception,[17] our Creator knows when and how best to communicate with each of us in ways that deepen our trust and shape our character. An integral part of our individual Christian growth is therefore learning about our self, growing in awareness of what our Creator and Father already knows. As Gary Thomas explains in his book *Sacred Pathways*, we each have particular 'spiritual temperaments'.[18] Deepening our appreciation of our tendencies and aptitudes in terms of encountering God and leaning into our preferences strengthens our quest to 'listen to God'. Wise saints of every era have recognised the importance of self-knowledge if we are to discern God's guidance: 'A humble self-knowledge is a surer way to God than a search after deep learning,' taught Thomas à Kempis; 'There is no deep knowing of God without deep knowing of self', wrote Calvin; Thomas Merton spoke of his desire 'to discover myself in discovering God'.

---

17 Jeremiah 1:5.
18 Thomas, G., 2000, *Sacred Pathways*, Grand Rapids, MI: Zondervan.

The early Irish Church drew particular inspiration from the posture of 'the beloved disciple' who *leaned* into Jesus at the Last Supper.[19] The image of that disciple, consciously pressing in close to Jesus, hanging on his every word, literally listening for the heartbeat of God, encouraged our ancestors to pursue practices of solitude, silence and contemplation. 'Pressing close' to Jesus and eagerly 'listening to God' will mean different things for each of us and a vital element of growing in faith is increasing our awareness of how that is manifest for each of us. That said, anyone who is serious about listening to God will soon learn why teachers of spirituality throughout history and across different traditions emphasise the value of gratitude as a practice that evokes an awareness of the divine and silence and solitude as a background that brings the divine voice into the foreground. When volunteers from diverse backgrounds, most not confessing Christians, participated in an eight-day silent retreat at Worth Abbey as part of the BBC series *The Big Silence*,[20] each one was thoroughly changed by the experience; the image and words of the man who identified himself as an atheist before the retreat, struggling some time later to express how God had spoken to him on the first day, has been lodged in my mind ever since.

The fact that Norwegian explorer Erling Kagge's *Silence*[21] became an instant bestseller in 2018 and has been published in thirty-three languages at the time of writing is an indication of the age of spiritual hunger we are living in. Interesting too is the recent boom of literature and resources promoting the practice and commending the benefits of gratitude, a powerful catalyst of spiritual awareness. At the heart of Thomas à Kempis's devotional masterpiece *The Imitation of Christ* is a call to learn to love our inseparable needs for solitude and silence. Perhaps one reason for the domestication of Christianity has been an emphasis on Christian community at the expense of solitary devotion, a focus on congregational life while

---

19 'Now there was leaning on Jesus' bosom one of his disciples, whom Jesus loved' (John 13:23 KJV).

20 www.bbc.co.uk/programmes/boovkk77.

21 Kagge, E., 2018, *Silence: In the Age of Noise*, London: Penguin.

neglecting the cultivation of the individual inner life. The two must grow together; one is a source of thriving for the other. As Dietrich Bonhoeffer warned: 'Let him [or her] who cannot be alone beware of community ... Let him [or her] who is not in community beware of being alone.'[22]

Selah

Pause. Reflect.

Finding out what he wants us to do and doing it – simple!

Just a few months after I first embraced the Christian faith I was fortunate to find myself in the study of a local church minister who was keen to help me grasp the basic foundations of faith in Christ and encourage me in the kind of habits that would enable me to grow as a Christian. The whole of one wall of his enormous study was lined, top to bottom, with what looked like well-read books and he began to enquire whether I had read this one or that one. As the answer in every case was 'no', he began to gather an armful of volumes from his collection and explain with prodigious enthusiasm why I might find each of them helpful in shaping my understanding and lifestyle. I appreciated his generosity, but, as I had recently finished four years of higher education, began to feel creeping discomfort at the idea that my recent decision to follow Jesus meant that I had enrolled on another course without realising it. I remember leaving his study with the unspoken thought, 'Surely all I need is to know what God wants me to do and then have the courage to do it.'

There is no doubt that the books that generous minister fed me over the following months had a transformative influence on me as a young Christian. And yet I also came to understand

22 Bonhoeffer, D., 1952, *Life Together*, New York, NY: Harper & Row, pp. 77–8.

that my initial thoughts were not far off the mark. As individuals we need to learn how it is that we hear God's voice and how to find the courage to respond in obedience. As groups of disciples together, whether that is as a local church congregation or as any other gathering that forms part of the 'one, holy, catholic and apostolic Church', we need to learn how we listen together, develop a shared understanding of what God is calling us to be and do, and how to best organise ourselves to that end.

The vital importance of this corporate listening is reinforced and highlighted when we consider the characteristics of congregations that are thriving. Back in the 1990s, Robert Warren was the Church of England's National Officer for Evangelism when it came to his attention that a number of congregations in Durham Diocese seemed to be flourishing and experiencing numerical growth while the majority in the same area were struggling and in decline. On closer investigation it became clear that the blossoming congregations, although different in many ways (small and large, urban and rural, various demographic profiles, etc.), had certain characteristics in common. These shared features were subsequently developed into what Warren dubbed the 'seven marks of healthy church'.[23]

As someone who has an adverse reaction to books and courses that appear to suggest a programmatic approach to faith development, *The Healthy Church Handbook* could easily have slipped under my radar. However, the captivating feature of the 'marks' that Warren highlighted is that together they closely resemble the values that Christ himself articulated and displayed in his life and teaching. Some are obvious and would constitute widely understood 'good practice' for Christian fellowship: the congregations Warren studied were 'energised by faith', inclusive, relational and willing to face the costs of change and growth. However, it was the third 'mark of healthy church' that caught my attention. Those congregations that appeared to be thriving had all learned to 'Seek to find out what God wants'. Warren and his team found that

---

23 Warren, R., 2012, *The Healthy Church Handbook*, London: Church House Publishing.

those congregations that determinedly pursued efforts to listen for God's guidance together – to 'discern the Spirit's leading rather than trying to please everyone' – were confident they were in step with God's purposes and consequently relaxed about what they were *not* doing.

Individually and corporately, we are called to a process of prayerful listening and devoted action. This is the rhythm of faithful following. Invitation and response: 'Follow me', Jesus said, ... 'and immediately they left and followed him'. We draw near and listen because of who he is. When the Supreme Court of the United States is in session, the entrance of the Justices into the Courtroom is announced by a marshal who calls out the words 'Oyez! Oyez! Oyez! All persons having business before the Honorable, the Supreme Court of the United States, are admonished *to draw near and give their attention*, for the Court is now sitting. God save the United States and this Honorable Court' (sic). While the word 'admonished' fails to express the affectionate tone of a loving Father, the sense of urging people to 'draw near and give their attention' is fitting. The Almighty Creator is eager for our attention. To call him Lord and then ignore him would seem rather odd. We never need approach with fear and yet, be under no illusion, to listen with open minds and obedient hearts is to step into the holy adventure of God's mission.

As my colleague Lesley Hamilton-Messer has observed, 'The trouble with listening is that you don't know what you're going to hear until it's too late.'[24] Listening is a threshold activity, a risky venture. Who knows where it will lead? Is this not the analogy that J. R. R. Tolkien is painting when we overhear his young adventurers reflecting on wisdom about 'the Road'? 'It's a dangerous business, Frodo, going out your door ... there's no knowing where you might be swept off to.'[25] We face a constant choice between a life of unconsidered momentum or listening – with the inherent risk of hearing ... well, who

---

24 McCarthy, D., 2019, *Seeing Afresh: Learning from Fresh Expressions of Church*, Edinburgh: Saint Andrew Press, p. 114.

25 Tolkien, J. R. R., 1993, *The Lord of the Rings Trilogy*, Boston, MA: Houghton Mifflin, Book 1 (The Fellowship of the Ring), p. 87.

knows what. We are constantly opting for familiarity or for liminality. The latter is not the opposite of the former, but is openness to the possibility of change. We either learn to listen to God or we settle for doing our own thing.

Let's not fool ourselves: to pursue a preconceived idea of 'church' without sincere listening is to ignore our fundamental purpose for being. How can the body function without reference to the head? As Eugene Peterson has observed, 'We are always coming in on something that is already going on ... long before I arrive on the scene, the Spirit is at work ... I must fit into what is already going on.'[26] How can we 'fit in' without listening? The vital heartbeat of the Church is the rhythm of listening and responding. In the world of nature, 'conservation' has often focused on 'preserving the little we've got left'; in contrast, rewilding allows biological powers to shape the environment of the future. In the world of the Church, the temptation to keep congregations happy and maintain the services, programmes and rotas can be hard to resist, but rewilding involves discerning God's mission and participating in what we discover. Rewilding moves beyond a sense of duty to perpetuate institutions and seeks to engage with the coming of the kingdom that is already at hand. 'The church doesn't exist for itself ... It is not ultimately about the church; it's about the people God wants to bless through the church. When the church loses sight of this, it loses its heart.'[27] When it recaptures sight of this, rewilding begins.

Selah

Stop. Listen. Pray.

---

26 Peterson, E., 1992, *Under the Unpredictable Plant*, Grand Rapids, MI: Eerdmans, p. 133.

27 Bell, R., 2005, *Velvet Elvis*, London: HarperCollins, p. 165.

Watching the sower, listening to the soil

Just as Jesus invites us 'Follow me', he also instructs us to observe 'the farmer'.[28] It is not any farmer; it is *the* farmer. We find the farmer at work and he is sowing. This is nothing like the precision seeding or hydroseeding of modern high-tech agro-business. The farmer we are instructed to watch engages in 'broadcast' sowing, the generous and extensive scattering of seed by hand. While we are told to look to the sower, Jesus' words soon draw our attention to the soil. The stories that Jesus tells next all begin, 'the kingdom of heaven is like ...', but that preface is absent here, because he is describing how the kingdom *begins*. 'The kingdom comes when the soil and the seed get together';[29] it is the impact of the gospel in a particular context, whether that is a life or a community.

It is impossible to overestimate the importance of the kingdom in Jesus' teaching. In Matthew's Gospel he refers to it more than forty times. It was the subject of his first sermon and we are told that it is what we should 'seek first'. The kingdom is to be a primary focus in our praying: 'your kingdom come'. For a lesser teacher the explanation of something so multi-faceted and paradoxical would be unachievable. The kingdom is 'now' and 'coming'; it is something that we are to 'seek' and something that we are invited to 'enter'. When Jesus says 'the kingdom of heaven is like ...' it is never followed by a simple formula. Rather, the genius storyteller weaves another unforgettable and compelling parable. Sometimes it is little more than a mini metaphor, a mustard seed; at other times, it is a full-blown narrative with plot, staging and cast. Occasionally the authoritative interpretation is on the lips of the teller, but usually we are left to figure it out. Whichever way understanding comes, we are left with personal implications to contend with. We are never left unaffected.

---

28 The Parable of the Sower or Parable of the Soils is found in the three synoptic Gospels: Matthew 13:1–23, Mark 4:1–20 and Luke 8:4–15.

29 Green, M., 2000, *The Message of Matthew*, London: IVP, p. 156.

The soil is the vital context of any rewilding, whether environmental or church. It is where the action happens. The kingdom is 'a marriage of seed and soil'.[30] So you can never afford to treat soil like dirt. Ask any gardener, any farmer. You may have premium seed and wonderful weather, but without good soil your highest horticultural hopes will be frustrated. Good soil is the legacy of how it is treated over the long term. When the soil is exploited, the future is grim. In 2014 the findings of UN research on soil degradation grabbed headlines around the world. 'Only 60 Years of Farming Left If Soil Degradation Continues' warned an article in the *Scientific American*.[31] A study in the UK found matters to be little better, estimating 'Only 100 harvests left in UK farm soils'.[32] A Sanskrit text written about 3,500 years ago highlights what we are relearning: 'Upon this handful of soil our survival depends. Husband it and it will grow our food, our fuel and our shelter and surround us with beauty. Abuse it and the soil will collapse and die, taking humanity with it.'[33] There can be no doubting the quality of the seed in Jesus' story and adverse climatic conditions are blamed for nothing. It's all down to the soil. We are taught that context matters.

For anyone who cares about the health and growth of the Church, listening to context is vital. Writing about the creation of new Christian communities, planting 'fresh expressions' of the Church, Michael Moynagh explains that 'Listening involves prayerfully attending to the context ... [it] is shorthand for the learning that occurs through conversations, observation, experience, background reading and sometimes more formal

---

30 Green, *Matthew*, p. 156.

31 Arsenault, C., 2014, 'Only 60 years of farming left if soil degradation continues', *Scientific American*, www.scientificamerican.com/article/only-60-years-of-farming-left-if-soil-degradation-continues/ (accessed 03.12.2019).

32 www.fwi.co.uk/news/only-100-harvests-left-in-uk-farm-soils-scientists-warn (accessed 27.11.2019).

33 Quoted in Monbiot, G., 2015, 'We're treating soil like dirt. It's a fatal mistake, as our lives depend on it', 25 March, *The Guardian*, www.theguardian.com/commentisfree/2015/mar/25/treating-soil-like-dirt-fatal-mistake-human-life (accessed 18.12.2019).

research.'[34] Jesus drew his hearers' attention to the long strip fields by the lakeside. Between each ribbon of soil there were rights of way, paths worn flint-hard by the passing of many sandals. Without the kind of 'natural disturbance' that broke open the exhausted ground of the Knepp Estate, the seed is unlikely to penetrate this hard shell. The 'rocky places' in Jesus' words comprised shallow soil on underlying limestone shelves. It was the first soil to warm up, ideal for rapid germination, but roots soon met an invisible and impenetrable barrier. The Parable of the Soils tells us that anyone concerned about the kingdom needs to pay careful attention to context.

A vigorous, sustainable landscape reflects its soil and climate and healthy, vibrant expressions of the Church are an authentic interaction between the message of Jesus and a specific time and place. They don't *mimic* their context, of course. While the gospel may lead to the celebration and thriving of some aspects of a cultural context, it will challenge and transform others. It is sometimes culture affirming and it is often countercultural, but one way or another what emerges is always shaped by context. Hence we need to know and understand the soil in which we live and into which the gospel is sown. Jesus' invitation to observe the sower is a call to engage in 'empirical theology'. That may sound like academic gibberish, but it simply means to gather evidence and to ask what God is revealing through it. 'Look,' Jesus says, 'look at the different contexts and see how the yield is different.' That is empirical theology. Indeed, one noted empirical theologian, Leslie Francis, suggests that when we look at the data relating to how people are responding to the gospel message across the UK, we can identify three kinds of 'soil'.[35] The first comprises people whose lives 'have been infused and transformed by the Christian narrative'. These are people whose lives and characters are undergoing the transformation into ever greater Christlikeness that comes from active following after Jesus. Professor Francis, drawing on a wealth of research data, confirms what many people already conclude

34 Moynagh, M., 2017, *Church in Life*, London: SCM Press, p. 320.
35 Francis, L., 2015, 'Taking discipleship learning seriously: setting priorities for the rural Church', *Rural Theology*, 13(1), pp. 18–30.

on the basis of their own personal observations and anecdotal evidence: 'such people are not as plentiful as we would like ... [they] are aging and not being replaced by a younger generation'.[36]

The second type of soil Francis identifies comprises people who 'have heard the Christian narrative, who have been exposed to the great Christian doctrines and who have experienced the liturgy of the church, but whose lives have not been transformed by the experience'.[37] These, then, are people who have actively opted for a different worldview. This soil too is less plentiful that it once was. But before we rejoice that the number of people who have encountered Church but not devoted themselves to Jesus is diminishing, we need to understand why. As Francis observes, many people in recent generations 'have not been sufficiently exposed to the Christian narrative to rebel against it'.[38] Having suggested that a third soil type represents those who know insufficient of the Christian gospel to enable a response, Francis goes on to identify similarities between the environment that Jesus and his first disciples encountered and that in which we find ourselves today. At this general level, there are people who are responding positively to the message, there are those who have rejected it, and there are others who are, as yet, unaware of the message. It's a helpful and thought-provoking framework and makes a strong case for prioritising strategies for communicating the message of Jesus to the growing proportion of the population who have yet to receive an opportunity to understand and respond. However, even at this macro level it is important to note that the picture does not easily translate to the relationship people have or do not have with local church congregations.

The picture Professor Francis outlines is complicated in at least two significant ways. First, it would be wrong to assume that a high level of commitment to church attendance and involvement is synonymous with the first soil type – that is, 'people whose hearts, minds and souls have been formed in

---

36 Francis, 'Taking discipleship learning seriously', p. 20.
37 Francis, 'Taking discipleship learning seriously', p. 20.
38 Francis, 'Taking discipleship learning seriously', p. 20.

Christ'.[39] Linda Woodhead's rigorous research among people across the UK who identify themselves as 'Anglican' demonstrates that churchgoers are a diverse group in terms of how their faith impacts their beliefs, values and behaviour. In addition, she found that among non-churchgoers, 'Many believe and practise in similar ways to churchgoers.'[40] In addition, my own studies among people who identify themselves as Christian but who are not attending a local church congregation found that about half demonstrated a high level of 'religious devotion – relationship with and commitment to God'.[41] We should not expect to find church congregations comprised of one type nor expect all of one type to respond in the same way in terms of involvement with local congregations or otherwise. When we listen to the context we realise that the idea of a local congregation of devoted disciples reaching out to a surrounding world comprising unbelieving non-churchgoers, who when they respond to Christ will then become committed members of a local congregation, is worse than simplistic; it bears little similarity to the twenty-first-century Church in the Western world.

Listening *together*

Paragliding is not usually a team sport, but as morning flying conditions develop and pilots decide when to take off, launch sites are abuzz with discussion of what the air is doing. To the untrained eye, air is invisible, but to the avid pilot of anything without an engine, the sky is rich with texture and meaning and the ground provides a patchwork of clues and signs. If all that is desired is to float gently from launch to landing, an

---

39 Francis, 'Taking discipleship learning seriously', p. 19.

40 Woodhead, L., 2013, '"Nominals" are the Church's hidden strength', *The Church Times*, www.churchtimes.co.uk/articles/2013/26-april/comment/opinion/nominals-are-the-church-s-hidden-strength (accessed 14.05.20).

41 Aisthorpe, S., 2014, 'A survey of Christians in the Highlands and Islands who are not part of a church congregation', *Rural Theology*, November, 12(2), pp. 83–95.

early morning take-off will provide a smooth glide. However, most pilots want to *fly*, they want to seek out the lift provided by thermals. This is the topic of intense conversation as pilots point to possible indications of rising air and weigh up their relative merits. Are there any dark surfaces down in the valley catching the sunshine? A car park, corrugated iron roof or ploughed field perhaps? If so, these will heat up faster than their surroundings, creating a bubble or column of warmer air. Fluttering leaves on a windless day provide tell-tale signs of thermal activity. Of course the local pilots will know best and the most experienced of all will be birds! Soaring birds make the invisible visible. All these signs, their interactions, and the impact of the wind and clouds, will be enthusiastically discussed by a gaggle of excited pilots, as, together, they determine what is happening and decide how they might interact with it.

As we travel together on the Jesus way, we need to listen *together*. Like reading the sky, we need to *learn* the skills of corporate listening, discernment based on the knowledge, insights, intuition and spiritual intelligence of a community. 'My sheep listen to my voice', Jesus said.[42] His invitation calls us into a new relationship ('I know them') and our response takes us in a new direction ('they follow me'). In the same way that Elisha prayed for his servant, we pray for one another to be companions (literally, those who share bread) with a shared vision:

> When an attendant of the man of God rose early in the morning and went out, an army with horses and chariots was all around the city. His servant said, 'Alas, master! What shall we do?' He replied, 'Do not be afraid, for there are more with us than there are with them.' Then Elisha prayed: 'O Lord, please open his eyes that he may see.' So the Lord opened the eyes of the servant, and he saw; the mountain was full of horses and chariots of fire all around Elisha.[43]

---

42 John 10:27.
43 2 Kings 6:15–17.

A substantial part of my day job for the last decade or so has been the great responsibility and privilege of helping church congregations and Christian groups in Scotland to 'listen together'. Through a series of retreats, workshops or conferences we listen to the context, studying the characteristics of the wider community; we look at who God has brought together at this particular time, the gifts, passions and resources of the congregation; we reflect on Scripture, practise deep listening to one another and, crucially, we seek to go beyond the purely rational and invite God to use our imaginations, to show a vision of the kingdom manifested in the coming years.[44] When a huddle of still earth-bound paraglider pilots look at the sky with longing, their minds and conversations move beyond the hard science of meteorology and fluid dynamics; they dream. In their imaginations they feel the abrupt turbulence as they cross from sinking air into a rising current. In their minds they are travelling across the sky and being drawn upwards by one thermal after another. This is not just wishful thinking, they are combining all the clues that their five senses perceive with their shared experience, and seeing possibilities. Then they launch. They test their hypotheses. As they soar through the space they have carefully considered from a hillside, new signs emerge: sometimes the smell of a farmyard far below tells them where that particular air originated, perhaps a piece of straw rising past them will give away the presence of uplift, maybe some spiralling birds will move on, encouraging them to follow.

For some, engaging the imagination in considering the future of the Church is a scary prospect. Surely it is an open invitation for unchecked ideas, lighting the fuse on whatever madcap, wacky or extreme notions might be lurking in a congregation? And yet it is this risk that highlights one reason why we need one another. It is as we come *together*, in a spirit of prayer, centred on Jesus, mindful of our identity as part of his Church,

---

44 For tools and techniques for facilitating these kinds of discerning activities with congregations and groups, and guidance for those involved in facilitating, see Aisthorpe, S. and colleagues, 2019, *Building The Body: Learning Activities for Growing Churches*, Edinburgh: Saint Andrew Press.

eager to hear through one another, that we can discern what God is showing *us*. 'If God's future carries new possibilities in its womb, through the Spirit prayerful imagination is the midwife that brings these possibilities to birth.'[45] In practice, when there is wide participation and commitment to prayerful listening, consensus develops and creates a shared vision. Like that physics experiment in school when a tuning fork is struck and another in a different part of the same room begins to vibrate, it seems that as we seek the same Spirit together, a unifying resonance results.

Then, like the paraglider pilots, it is time to launch and, continuing in an attitude of listening and learning, no longer earthbound and tied to the present, but airborne and actively pursuing a vision of the future, we act on what we have heard. It is this rhythm of listening and trusting, of discerning and doing, an intensely collaborative and prayerful movement, which is at the heart of rewilding the Church.

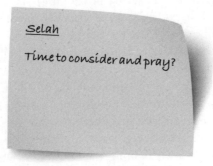

Selah

Time to consider and pray?

---

45 Moynagh, M., 2017, *Church in Life*, London: SCM Press, p. 321.

6

SIMPLIFY: Learning to Travel Light

'Don't load yourselves up with equipment.
Keep it simple; you are the equipment.'
Luke 9:3 (MSG)

Keep it simple

Simplicity.

It's such a beautiful word that I just want to allow it to have its own line, uncluttered by any additional words! Great names of every era, leaders in their fields of science, literature, religion and philosophy, have concluded that, quite apart from the practical paybacks of simplicity, truth and goodness are characterised by an essential simplicity. For Francis de Sales, seventeenth-century Bishop of Geneva, whose reflections on spiritual direction inform and enlighten much contemporary writing on faith formation, simplicity was a vital characteristic of healthy Christian living. 'In everything, love simplicity', he urged. 'I recommend to you holy simplicity.'[1] Operating in a totally different era and field of endeavour, Ernst Schumacher, the twentieth-century statistician and economist, countered modernisation and ever-expanding economies of scale with a plea for courageous leaders to recognise the benefits of simplicity. Polymaths and geniuses of every generation, the likes of Einstein, Newton and Da Vinci, have recognised that the search for truth tends to turn towards simplicity.

---

1 Quoted in Foster, R., 1987, *Freedom of Simplicity*, London: Triangle, p. 52.

Like breaking through into a spacious glade after cutting a trail through dense undergrowth, the discovery of genuine simplicity comes as a hard-won revelation, only uncovered after considerable toil. The simplicity commended by the brightest minds and the greatest souls of the ages is neither unconsidered nor the fruit of laziness. In the words of inventor Oliver Wendell Holmes: 'For simplicity on this side of complexity I would not give you a fig, but for simplicity on the other side of complexity, for that I would give you anything I have.'[2]

Few of us will ever embark on the kind of extreme experiment in simple living undertaken by American poet and philosopher Henry David Thoreau. In July 1845 he voluntarily exchanged his conventionally comfortable home for a simple hut on the edge of Walden Pond in Massachusetts – where he stayed for two years, two months and two days. Explaining the purpose of his radical choice, he wrote: 'I went to the woods because I wished to live deliberately, to front only the essential facts of life, and see if I could not learn what it had to teach, and not, when I came to die, discover that I had not lived.'[3]

And what did Thoreau learn? Well, his conclusions are captured in this selective summary from the classic account of his adventures in austerity: 'Our life is frittered away by detail ... Simplicity, simplicity, simplicity! I say, let your affairs be as two or three, and not a hundred or a thousand ... Simplify, simplify.'[4] Inspired by an impulse to determine for himself the impact of stripping away all but the essentials, he discovered the wisdom contained in that invocation of Jesus as he sent out his followers: 'Keep it simple.'[5] He learned by experience the vital benefits of living minimally and uncovered an antidote for the malaise that King Solomon had recognised many centuries

---

2 Quoted in Jamieson, A., 2002, *A Churchless Faith*, London: SPCK, p. 138.

3 Thoreau, H., 1854, *Walden*, https://wwnorton.com/college/history/america-essential-learning/docs/HDThoreau-Walden-1854.pdf, p. 46 (accessed 18.07.2019).

4 Thoreau, *Walden*, p. 46.

5 Luke 9:3 (MSG).

previously: 'This is all that I have learned: God made us plain and simple, but we have made ourselves very complicated.'[6]

It is tempting to imagine that the societies and the times in which the characters of the biblical narrative lived were so simple that the dangers related to material accumulation and mental clutter would be greatly diminished compared to our own day. Surely the need to embark on a pathway towards greater simplicity is a relatively recent thing – therapy for people deprived of silence by the buzz of traffic; whose attention is robbed by technology? Certainly there is a burgeoning of modern fads that promise a return to simplicity: Marie Kondo has sparked a movement of decluttering consultants, offering 'inner peace through freedom from clutter'; 'self-storage' facilities have mushroomed around the fringes of our towns and cities, offering the possibility of clutter-free homes without the tough decisions involved in authentic simplification. However, it is impossible to undertake a serious reading of Scripture without being struck by the extreme gravity of its authors' urgings to flee the psychotic lust for affluence and the toxic tendency towards ever-greater complexity. Jesus identified the Aramaic word for wealth, 'mammon', as being a direct rival to God. A desire for one is so completely incompatible with a desire for the other, that he depicted them as being like oil and water or, in his own analogy, like a servant being torn between the demands of two irreconcilable masters. According to Jesus, the person who attempts to please both is inevitably destined to end up hating one and loving the other, being devoted to one and despising the other.[7]

In contrast to material accumulation and increasingly convoluted organisations, the life of Jesus was one of extreme simplicity. In the words of Richard Foster, author and teacher of Christian spirituality: 'The witness to simplicity is profoundly rooted in the biblical tradition, and most perfectly exemplified in the life of Jesus Christ.'[8] With his roots in the Quaker tradition, Foster's passion for simplicity is no surprise,

---

6 Ecclesiastes 7:29 (GNT).
7 Luke 16:13.
8 Foster, *Freedom of Simplicity*, p. 3.

but one might not expect the same sentiments to be shared by the leader of the world's largest and longest functioning institution. However, in his autobiography, the head of the Catholic Church at its numerical peak, Pope John XXIII, wrote of his 'desire to simplify all that is complicated'.[9]

Perhaps, at some subconscious level, the fact that the great debates within the life of the Christian community tend to focus on matters about which Jesus said little or nothing is a way of evading matters about which he said a great deal. The relative neglect of his teaching on wealth and material accumulation is a case in point. Surely a faithful response to that simple invitation 'Follow me' includes ethical implications so fundamental and far-reaching that some behaviours that contemporary society celebrates, such as slavery to brand and fashion, must also be recognised as 'invasive species' in any desire to rewild the Church.

The *outcome* of rewilding is complex. Landscape becomes more multidimensional, biodiversity becomes richer. However, as a policy it is simple, an approach rooted in trust. As an ecological strategy we trust that nature knows best; in rewilding the Church we rely on God's power and wisdom and are suspicious of substitutes; both rewilded landscape and rewilded Church emerge from the Creator's hand. Simplicity is what allows us to respond to Jesus' call 'Follow me' with the minimum of interference. The rules of life of monastic traditions throughout history vary in many ways, but simplicity is always there, creating the space for transformation to occur. It distressed Jesus that people had taken God's law and woven it into a web of onerous regulation, far removed from its loving intentions.[10] If we want an example of simplicity, how about 'love God and love your neighbour'.[11] As with rewilding in nature, the consequence of *this* kind of simplicity will be rich and complex, beautiful, demanding and compelling. Simplicity is not an out-

---

9 Pope John XXIII, 1965, *Journal of a Soul*, D. White (trans.), London: Chapman. Quoted in Foster, *Freedom of Simplicity*, p. 5.

10 Luke 11:42; Matthew 23:23.

11 Matthew 22:36–40.

come, but is the kind of context that facilitates and optimises God's work, minimising distractions and diversions.

Travel light

Parallel passages to Luke's account of Jesus sending out the Twelve quoted at the beginning of this chapter are found in Matthew and Mark's Gospels too. The details differ. According to Mark, the Disciples may take a staff, wear sandals, but not carry an extra garment. Luke prohibits a staff, a means of protection and a 'just in case' for injuries along the way. Matthew is clear that no money is to be taken and the absence of a bag will ensure that they cannot carry other supplies. However, while the specifics vary, the gist is clear and Eugene Peterson's idiomatic translation of Matthew's version expresses it with exquisite and apposite simplicity: 'Travel light.'

Whether it's an Olympic sprint, a dash to the bus stop or a long-distance pilgrimage, Jesus' advice to 'travel light' is astute. Just how wise this instruction is, I learned the hard way. It was 1984. A friend and I had travelled to Norway to achieve a long-held ambition of making an ascent of the Troll Wall, Europe's tallest rock face. During the first two weeks of continuous rainfall a dense fog hung low and heavy over the wall. We didn't even catch a glimpse of our objective. Then, when the veil of cloud finally lifted, it was clear from the roaring of waterfalls and rumbling of rockfall that it would be some time before our north-facing dream would be in climbable condition. Frustrated and determined to climb something, we turned our attentions to some of the smaller, but still imposing, cliffs on the opposite side of the valley. Being south facing we reckoned that these would be dry and safe considerably sooner than our main objective. In particular, the South Pillar of Mongejura caught our attention. Sweeping up for 3,000 vertical feet from the valley floor, it bathed in every hour of sunshine available. Based on the scant information available, it seemed wise to pack for two days. Our idea was that whoever took the lead would climb unencumbered and then the one climbing second, enjoying the security of a rope from above, would carry a ruck-sack containing food, water and sleeping bags.

Ah, 'the best laid plans'! Although the actual climbing proved to be well within our capabilities, the task of climbing second with what we had deemed essential proved to be both gruel-ling in the extreme and painfully slow. It was like the hare and the tortoise, tied together in a comical vertical race. Whoever was leading would gallop up to the next ledge and arrange an anchor. Then the second, the heavily burdened tortoise, would toil and thrutch, heave and grovel, lunge and lurch in a vertical crawl, straining to emulate the leader's progress, until they arrived breathless and exhausted at the leader's perch.

After a few rope lengths of this painful palaver, the comedy was in danger of becoming a tragedy. A council of war was convened. Balanced on an overhanging prow, with acres of steep granite stretching above and substantially less below, we knew that something would have to change. We could con-tinue in the same fashion, knowing that at the current rate of progress we would need more time than estimated and, as a result, would face an ordeal with serious hunger and thirst. Or we could beat a retreat. In fact, abseiling down what we had worked so hard to climb wouldn't take long at all, so poor had been our upward progress. We could be home for tea.

However, there was also another option. We could switch to the approach that we now realised we should have adopted in the first place. We could abandon our heavy load, cut ourselves free from the burden that had become a ball and chain, imped-ing our progress – and make a dash for the top. By doing so we would be experiencing the reason we were there. We would be climbing, unimpeded. And that's what we did. We cast aside what we had convinced ourselves was indispensable, but had turned out to be an encumbrance. Unburdened, we quickly fell into a rhythm. Unencumbered, our sluggish struggle soon became a joyful flow. The long days of northern summers meant that arriving on the summit in late evening was not a problem and, after a long descent down a scree-filled gully, we surprised our friends by stumbling back into camp in the early hours, ear-to-ear smiles splitting our weary faces.

A week later, each carrying a single litre of water, a few snacks, a sweater and survival bag, we finally got to grips with the Troll Wall, Europe's so-called 'Vertical Mile'. No doubt, if we'd tackled it without the hard-won lesson to 'travel light' behind us, our efforts would have led to a humiliating defeat on our ambition for the summer. As it turned out, the learning from that previous climb, 'keep it simple ... travel light', made for a trouble-free ascent and an experience that reinforced a commitment to travelling light.

A concerted call

In my work with local churches, as one element of workshops, retreats and conferences designed to re-envision and plan for the next chapter of the congregation's life, I often use the Gospel accounts of Jesus sending out the Twelve in a kind of corporate reflection or '*Lectio Divina*'.[12] The same passage is read several times during the day and participants are invited to listen in a slightly different way on each occasion. We sometimes read from different translations and avoid emphasising one part of the passage over others. During one reading participants are encouraged to listen for the whole sweep of the narrative, trying to avoid their minds being absorbed in any individual theme or phrase, focusing on following the whole rather than grasping any particular details. Another time they are instructed to have their 'spiritual antennae' up for any particular thought, word or phrase that seems to be highlighted for them. At some point we pray along the lines, 'Lord, is there anything here that speaks to us about our part in your mission?' Each person's reflections are private and remain confidential until towards the end of the process, when all are invited to consider whether they have insights that might be of relevance as we seek the

12 *Lectio Divina*, translated literally 'divine or sacred reading', is a way of interacting with Scripture that dates back to the earliest centuries of Christianity. It is traditionally undertaken as a community practice and comprises the four movements of reading, meditating, prayer and contemplation.

way ahead as a congregation. What has been striking is that, in recent years, whether we turn to Matthew's account (where the parallel verse to the one at the beginning of this chapter is rendered with appropriate simplicity, 'Travel light') or the Lucan version of events ('Keep it simple'), of the rich and eclectic array of themes in these passages, again and again the majority of people highlight the words 'Travel light' or 'Keep it simple' or express the same theme in their own words. It seems that at this time in the Church's history, this has become a prophetic word, a timely word for church congregations.

In addition to these voices from the few dozen congregations I have had the privilege to work with personally, the views of others well-placed to gain an overview of themes and trends within the denominations and networks of the Church add credence to the suggestion of a prophetic call. Former Principal Clerk of the Church of Scotland, Finlay Macdonald, understands the complexities and burdens of church life better than most people. The Principal Clerk is responsible for advising the Church's General Assembly, Moderator and those in positions of responsibility throughout the denomination on church law, practice and procedure. It is more than a decade since his own publication, *Confidence in a Changing Church*,[13] highlighted the excessive and needless proportion of its members' time consumed in 'keeping the system going'. More recently, leading theologian and visionary voice Doug Gay used the platform of the Chalmers Lectures[14] to echo the exasperated observations of the Very Revd Dr Macdonald, pointing to processes and procedures that are excessively expansive, unreasonably exhausting and expensive to boot. Having highlighted 'too many meetings, which consume too many people hours', the Revd Dr Doug Gay concluded that the Church is 'long overdue a moment of refocusing, of streamlining, of simplifying'.

---

13 Macdonald, F., 2004, *Confidence in a Changing Church*, Edinburgh: Saint Andrew Press.

14 2017, 'Lecture series ends with prophecy for the Kirk', www.churchofscotland.org.uk/news_and_events/news/2017/lecture_series_ends_with_prophecy_for_the_kirk (accessed 22.07.2019).

These are not voices from church-bashing critics; these are two devoted disciples of Christ who, for considerable chunks of their lives, have served their particular denomination and the wider Church in a variety of senior roles. It is from their perspective as loving insiders that they have expressed exasperation at the difficulty in achieving change and their longing for a season of simplification.

Regardless of denomination, the observations of leaders and senior staff seem to corroborate the perceptions of grassroots members: there is a craving for a simpler expression of Church. If further evidence of this ache for simplicity were required, it is found within the experiences of the multitude of Christians who are currently not connected with any local congregation. One of the stand-out themes from recent research projects among Christians who have disengaged from traditional church structures[15] is a longing for a less complicated form of fellowship, where the demands are those inherent in following Christ rather than burdens and stresses resultant from unnecessarily complex institutions. Throughout that research a hunger for something lighter is a recurring refrain; a longing for faith-based community where the focus on worship, mission and service is not drowned out by demands of administrative duties.

I remember the profound frustration and disappointment expressed by one of the interviewees in those studies, still devoted to following Jesus nearly two decades after leaving their congregation, as they explained how 'there was a request for more and more time to be spent on the mechanics of Presbyterianism ... and of course Presbyterianism is an amazingly well-designed machine in that it can keep going, keep going, keep going'. And be assured that for 'Presbyterianism' any other form of church polity could be substituted: this

---

15 Aisthorpe, S., 'Listening to and learning from Christians in the Highlands and Islands', DMin. dissertation, Glyndŵr University, 2016; Aisthorpe, S., 2014, 'A survey of Christians in the Highlands and Islands who are not part of a church congregation', *Rural Theology*, November 12(2), pp. 83–95; Faith in Scotland study, see Aisthorpe, S., 2016, *The Invisible Church*, Edinburgh: Saint Andrew Press, pp. 16–17.

frustration with institutional maintenance sucking the life out of Christians is experienced in historical denominations and contemporary networks, regardless of their theological persuasions and regardless of the style of their worship.

The particular person quoted above has founded a large and successful company and is someone whose expertise in establishing and managing effective businesses is widely sought. So he certainly does not have an aversion to corporate organisations in general. He knows the value of a healthy organisation both to those who work in it and those it serves. He knows that church does not need to be how it often is, and yet he also knows from painful experience that change in church congregations seems to be especially difficult to achieve. And he is not alone. 'Frustration with the change-resistant culture of congregations' was found to be a recurring theme in the interviews conducted in the study *Faith Journeys Beyond the Congregations* in Scotland.[16]

I remember the palpable sense of liberation and reassurance that was injected into a conference of regional church leaders when, referring to the regulatory complexities of the denomination, a senior officer of that church's central offices encouraged those present by saying: 'We have to remember that we made this stuff up, but we can always unmake too.' It was a wonderful sentiment and it is true. However, unfortunately it seems that 'unmaking stuff' in the context of church institutions is tremendously challenging.

Most of the historical denominations have a track record of determined undertakings to shed superfluous structures and redundant processes that struggle to do much 'unmaking'. And it is important to state that institutional arrangements that waste resources and erode enthusiasm are not the exclusive preserve of the 'traditional' churches either. Newer networks and 'independent' churches also recognise the apparently default process of rapid complexification and the development of risk-averse cultures that impede innovation. Among the interviewees who have recounted their experience of the soul-wrenching process

---

16 Aisthorpe, *The Invisible Church*, p. 105.

of disengaging from church congregations are those from all points of the ecclesiastical and theological spectrum.

The Holy Unbuilder

It may be tempting to dismiss these kinds of frustrations with institutional complexities out of hand. After all, who enjoys meetings for their own sake? Surely nobody wants unnecessary procedures or agencies, but any organisation or even the simplest gathering requires preparations to be made and entails a degree of management? However, the frustration comes from the sense that necessary administrative arrangements tend to, as one interviewee expressed, 'grow arms, legs and many other less useful protrusions'. Many organisations, whether commercial, social or charitable, have forces at work or processes of review and reform that keep them lean and fit for purpose. However, church institutions appear to develop unchecked until organisational charts struggle to express their convoluted nature. In the case of those that have been around for a long time, so great is the complexity that it takes talented legal minds to grasp the intricacies of their policies. Even the new kids on the ecclesiastical block seem to have a tendency to develop regulations that far exceed those required for good practice in areas such as charity governance, safeguarding, and health and safety – and, ironically, such complexity, rather than leading to good governance, tends to undermine compliance and lead to patterns of poor decision-making. While the words of Jesus, 'Keep it simple', would make an excellent introduction to a seminar on the principles of good governance, they do not spring to mind as a founding principle of the Christian Church. But they are.

In his allegorical story *The Carpenter and the Unbuilder*, David Greibner tells of a carpenter who received an astonishing invitation to visit the King. Of course he was keen to accept the King's invitation and set off. However, he was so intent on building safe places on his journey to the royal banquet that he kept forgetting all about the amazing purpose of the journey and the brilliance of the person he was invited to meet. His need for security and structure, his aversion to stepping out in simple trust, prevented him from responding to the King's beautiful invitation with unhindered passion. Eventually the King sent an 'Unbuilder' to remind the carpenter about the invitation and to urge him to resume his journey. The Unbuilder told the carpenter that the King was waiting for him. He showed him a simpler way to travel and demonstrated that it was not necessary to keep building new shelters along the way. The Unbuilder also commended an approach whereby the Carpenter would not need to stress over which path to take each day. By remembering what he knew about the King and the incredible love evident in the King's invitation, the Carpenter would come to a place where decision-making was straightforward: 'When you have remembered as clearly as you think you can, consider the paths that lie before you and see which seems to best satisfy your longing for, and remembering of, the King.' This practice served him well. Indeed, 'slowly it began to seem as though they were already on the journey' and 'with a deep sense of freedom they were off'.

Some may reject such an allegory as simplistic. However, does it not have a powerful resonance with our current situation? A people called by the King? Longing to respond to his beautiful invitation and yet constrained by unnecessary structures, risk-averse cultures and fear of getting things wrong? In the New Testament the Holy Spirit is often referred to as the *paraclete*, literally 'one who comes alongside'. A related word, *parakletos*, refers to an advocate in a court of law. So the Spirit comes alongside and is also *on* our side. Like the 'unbuilder', the Spirit of the King is calling us to a season of simplification. As Richard Foster puts it, 'Let us seek to do "ecclesiastical mercy-killing" wherever we can.'[17] Wherever we find ourselves within the echelons of the Church (and remember, there is only one Church despite many diverse expressions and the multiplicity of manmade divisions), we need to be alert to structures

---

17 Foster, *Freedom of Simplicity*, p. 161.

that have outlived their usefulness; committees and procedures that, while once beneficial, now distract or inhibit us from responding to the King. Even those for whom following Jesus does not currently involve any recognisable institution or organisation will benefit from asking the Holy Unbuilder to show any invasive species that hinder the rewilding process.

Selah

Pause. Reflect.

The trajectory of simplicity

When it came to writing the concluding chapter of *The Invisible Church*, I attempted to take a step back and, having considered the evidence related to the changing shape of the Church in the UK and reflected on the empirical data of congregations and of the 'invisible church', tried to discern some 'Glimpses of the Way Ahead'. In terms of the actual beliefs and the personal practices of individuals I was forced to conclude that change is gradual and that no one direction of travel is discernible. The evidence is contradictory. Various currents can be identified, but their interactions are complex and no single bearing can be discerned. Surveys in some denominations have indicated 'a growing liberal consensus within British churches as well as in British society';[18] the most recent church census in Scotland found a slight increase in congregations that were described by their leaders as 'Evangelical' (up to 40 per cent from 38 per cent in 1994);[19] long-term research into how biblical conservatism among Anglican clergy changes over time found that individuals, regardless of gender or age, tend to become

---

18 Randall, K., 2017, 'Are liberals winning? A longitudinal study of clergy churchmanship', *Journal of Empirical Theology*, 31(2), pp. 265–87.

19 www.brierleyconsultancy.com/scottish-church-census.

less conservative and more liberal over time.[20] The list goes on and the diversity of findings seems to broaden with every addition.

While the trends regarding any changes to the nature of people's faith are yet to become clearer, the way people express their faith *together*, or the trajectory in terms of the 'shape' that Christian community takes, is clearer: 'the evidence points to a reshaping, rebalancing or reconfiguration of the Church ... forms of Christian community which are highly organised are declining ... people who move away from church congregations are involved in fellowship which is informal and highly relational'.[21] God's rewilding of the Church is reflected in a simplification, a flourishing of the small and simple and the rapid decline of the large and the complex. Here then is one more example of where we should 'find out what God is doing and join in' as Rowan Williams has put it.[22] A rewilded landscape is the result of what takes root and flourishes. A rewilded Church emerges from what germinates and thrives when the 'keystone' is reintroduced and invasive species are culled, when the focus is on Jesus and that which entangles is cast aside. While the increasing interest in cathedral worship[23] is one of many indicators that large institutions will continue to have, an important part in the overall biodiversity that is the Church, there is no doubt that the overall balance is shifting towards the small and the simple.

Surely being Church, sharing the Christian journey together, even in the most uncomplicated way, demands a degree of organisation? While the answer is undoubtedly 'yes', there is a long spectrum between the kind of 'layers of bylaws and

---

20 Randall, 2017, 'Are liberals winning?'.

21 Aisthorpe, *Invisible Church*, pp. 194–5.

22 'Archbishop's Presidential Address – General Synod, York, July 2003', http://aoc2013.brix.fatbeehive.com/articles.php/1826/archbishops-presidential-address-general-synod-york-july-2003 (accessed 27.01. 2020).

23 Church of England Church Growth Research Programme, 2014, *From Anecdote to Evidence: Findings of the Church Growth Research Programme 2011–2013*, London: Church House Publishing, p. 19.

policies, often couched in archaic language, which only a few specialists really understand'[24] experienced in some denominations and the 'whose place are we meeting at next' level of organisation that characterises many small groups emerging from within the so-called invisible church.

In reflecting on questions of ecclesiastical simplicity, there are some important practical considerations. Perhaps the first is the direction of travel. Is the tendency towards simplicity or complexity? For those embroiled in complex structures, optimal simplicity tomorrow is not a possibility. However, by ensuring that Foster's 'ecclesiastical mercy-killings' are a feature of church life and making choices to resist unnecessary complexity, organisations can move towards greater simplicity. A second consideration is that, when it comes to groups of people sharing the Jesus way together, size is crucial. The difference in dynamics between cathedral and home group, cell and celebration are fundamental. While it is often in the context of larger gatherings, where it may not be possible to know each participant personally, that people experience the particular encouragement that comes from shared celebration, it is only in the small group that the deep sharing and profound mutuality, as insisted upon in the many 'one another' exhortations of the New Testament, is found and fostered. Of course that small group may or may not be part of a much larger association. The biggest church congregations in the world invariably devote careful attention to the small group experience of their members.

It is unsurprising then that empirical evidence shows that small churches are more likely to experience numerical growth than larger congregations. The findings of the Church of England's substantial 'Church Growth Research Programme' was unequivocal: 'Small churches (0–14 and 15–29) exhibit the most positive growth trends'.[25] While numerical growth is only one aspect of church growth, it is still an important

---

24 Aisthorpe, *The Invisible Church*, p. 195.
25 Church of England Church Growth Research Programme, *From Anecdote to Evidence*, p. 28.

indicator of health. It seems bizarre then that most denominations respond to shrinking congregations with a programme of amalgamations – despite the evidence in the same and similar research that 'There is a strong negative trend between the more churches amalgamated together and the likelihood of decline (across all categories of church size)'.[26] When the Institute for Natural Church Development (NCD) undertook the most extensive study of its kind and analysed more than four million survey responses from more than 70,000 church congregations worldwide, they concluded that of the 170 variables they investigated it was the presence of 'holistic small groups' that had the strongest positive relationship with numerical church growth. Also, where involvement in such groups ('which go beyond simple discussing Bible passages, to applying its spiritual message in daily life' and where 'group members are able to bring up issues and questions that are their immediate personal concerns'[27]) is viewed as more important than participation in congregational worship, there was an especially strong link with both numerical growth and high scoring on the NCD congregational health 'quality index'.

The empirical case supports the theological argument for the relational benefits and missional effectiveness of church expressed as small groups. Optimal group size and dynamics are those that facilitate the kinds of 'one anothering' of one another that grow what the New Testament calls *koinonia*, but which also enable people to continue to be 'in the world', engaged with 'the rest of life'. Reflecting on the imperative of developing a sensitivity to the work of the Holy Spirit in oneself and others, Anglican Bishop John Taylor concludes that 'the ideal shape of the church ... will provide this "one-another-ness"' with 'the least possible withdrawal of Christians from their corporateness with their fellow men in the world'. Indeed he goes on to advocate church expressed in 'little con-

---

26 Church of England Church Growth Research Programme, *From Anecdote to Evidence*, p. 28.

27 Schwarz, C., 1996, *Natural Church Development: A Guide to Eight Essential Qualities of Healthy Churches*, St Charles, IL: Churchsmart Resources, p. 32.

gregations'. Rewilding the Church will involve a revolution of small things. It is such simple expressions of Church that Taylor advocated 'must become normative if the church is to respond to the Spirit's movement in the life of the world'.[28]

Selah

Take a moment to consider.

---

28 Taylor, J., 1972, *The Go-Between God*, London: SCM Press, quoted in Bradbury, P., 2019, *Home By Another Route*, Abingdon: Bible Reading Fellowship, p. 77.

7

SEEK: Noticing Who's Missing

'... does he not leave the ninety-nine on the mountains
and go in search of the one that went astray?'
Matthew 18:12

Lessons from returnees

Surely these are the most magnificent birds in the UK. With
their broad, ragged wings spanning more than two metres
and powerful talons capable of snatching a mountain hare or
a substantial fish, the sight of a white-tailed eagle cruising a
craggy escarpment for prey is one of nature's most stunning
spectacles. So arresting is the huge area of their wings that they
have been dubbed 'the flying barn door';[1] so striking are their
piercing golden eyes that in Gaelic they are known as *iolaire
suile na grèine*, literally 'the eagle with the sunlit eye'.[2] When
I was a teenager, my favourite bird book recorded them as a
'rare winter visitor from Scandinavia'.[3] I never seriously enter-
tained the possibility of ever encountering one in the wild in
the UK.

Then these majestic creatures were reintroduced to the west
coast of Scotland in the 1970s and later to the east coast in
the 2000s. Field guides and books about British birds caught
up with developments and explained that, while still an
endangered species, these rare raptors could be found on the

---

1 2009, '"Flying barn doors" land in Fife', *BBC News*, http://news.
bbc.co.uk/1/hi/scotland/edinburgh_and_east/8119508.stm (accessed 05.
12.2019).

2 https://www.stornowaygazette.co.uk/news/return-of-the-sea-
eagle-1-2810327 (accessed 05.12.2019).

3 The Reader's Digest, 1980, *Book of British Birds*, London: Drive
Publications, p. 271.

Isle of Skye, Rum, Mull and several other sites on the west coast. The widespread understanding among ornithologists was that these were a species that inhabited wild craggy coastlines and rugged mountains. So it came as something of a surprise to many when the latest reintroduction programme was announced as being centred on the Isle of Wight,[4] an island of chalk downland on England's southern coast and at the edge of the world's busiest shipping route. While the fact that we persecuted them to extinction in Scotland in the early twentieth century was well known, we have generally lost sight of more ancient times when they thrived throughout the UK. They were once widespread along the whole of the South Coast of England and Natural England's decision to bring back this iconic species to the area is beginning where the last known pair to breed in England died in 1780. For those with eyes to see, place names containing the Germanic word 'erne' (meaning eagle) reveal that our ancient ancestors associated certain villages and towns scattered across much of lowland Britain and Ireland with the white tailed eagle.[5] The *Anglo-Saxon Chronicle* entry for AD 937 ends its description of the Battle of Brunanburh by saying that, along with wolves and ravens, white tailed eagles feasted on the battlefield.[6] We played the main role in the extinction from our islands of these awe-inspiring birds and are now helping to bring them back from the brink.

Despite the challenges of agro-chemicals and some continued persecution, where these eagles have been reintroduced, they are thriving. They are demonstrating that they, along with many other species, are capable of living in a wider variety of landscapes and ecosystems than we previously thought

---

4 Diamond, J., 2019, 'Natural England issues licence to release white-tailed eagles', Natural England, *Gov.uk*, https://naturalengland. blog.gov.uk/2019/04/02/natural-england-issues-licence-to-release-white-tailed-eagles/ (accessed 06.12.2019).

5 For dozens of examples from across the whole of the United Kingdom and Ireland, see Yalden, D., 2007, 'The older history of the White-tailed Eagle in Britain', *British Birds*, August, 100, pp. 471–80.

6 Yalden, D. and U. Albarella, 2010, *The History of British Birds*, Oxford: Oxford University Press, p. 124.

possible. Indeed, environmental scientists have noticed that many species are challenging our previous assumptions about their habitat range. An article with an unusually eye-catching title for an academic journal appeared in *Current Biology* in 2018. The authors of 'Are the ghosts of nature's past haunting ecology today?'[7] argue that recorded occurrences of animals outside their usual habitat, previously written off as serendipitous sightings of the unusual behaviour of a few quirky individuals, actually point to something far more significant. From mountain lions wandering around grasslands to wolves moving into coastal regions and freshwater alligators expanding their habitats into saltwater areas, animals are forcing us to question our ideas about what their 'normal' habitats are. Recent research shows that following long-term protection, from sea otters to orang-utans, many species are being found in habitats that were until recently considered beyond their 'niche space'. In the cases of some organisms, what we thought was 'normal habitat' as a matter of necessity or preference seems to be their refuge of last resort, where they have been forced to live. 'Historical records, surveys of protected areas and patterns of animals moving into habitats that were former hunting hotspots, indicate that – rather than occupying them for the first time – many of these animals are in fact recolonizing ecosystems.'[8]

As well as reconsidering what constitutes 'home' for particular species, we also need to think again about the variety of organisms that constitute the normal range of species in particular landscapes and ecosystems. Where rewilding is allowed to occur there will be surprises, some of which will remind us of ages past as apparent strangers turn out to be returnees. For the human inhabitants of the Isle of Wight white tailed eagles are new additions to the population. However, for the area's

---

7 Silliman, B. and colleagues, 2018, 'Are the ghosts of nature's past haunting ecology today?', *Current Biology*, 28(9), www.researchgate.net/publication/324999795_Are_the_ghosts_of_nature's_past_haunting_ecology_today, pp. 532–7 (accessed 06.12.2019).

8 Silliman and colleagues, 2018, 'Are the ghosts of nature's past', p. 532.

most ancient trees, some of which might become their new homes, they are returning friends after a temporary absence.

In recent times in the Christian community we have tended to see the local church congregation as the 'normal habitat' of those who follow Jesus, but new data shows that this is no longer the case.[9] Just as mountain lions and orang-utans are challenging our understanding of where they can thrive, so evidence from our longitudinal study of so-called churchless Christians is demonstrating that the variety of habitats in which Christians are flourishing is considerable. In addition, just as our deepening awareness reveals that landscapes we considered complete and well-rounded may be missing key species, so our growing understanding of Christian congregations, groups and institutions is highlighting significant absences and gaps.

Some of these gaps, these missing ones, are obvious. Many congregations mourn the absence of certain groups – for example, young people, men or those from particular ethnic groups within their area. However, other aspects of a group's 'biodiversity' are just as influential as gender, generation and ethnicity in terms of shaping responses to the invitation of Jesus and how we experience and express our faith, but are invisible and usually unconsidered. As followers of Jesus we are all *homo sapiens* and members of the same sub-group, *homo sapiens christiana* perhaps, but there is considerable diversity among us. These differences shape the way we see the world, how we understand Christianity and how we express our life in Christ. When researchers explore the Christian community in its various expressions it becomes clear that some 'strains' of Christian are commonplace, dominating their particular habitat, and others are found only rarely. In this chapter we will encounter some 'types' of people that are so rare in the

---

9 When we talk about 'habitat' we tend to mean the whole operating environment of an organism and of course no expression of Church is ever that. Even for those who are most devoted to and involved in a local congregation, church-related activity fills a minority of their time. However, there has been a dramatic shift among the Christian population away from 'habitats' centred on institutional expressions of Church.

traditional habitat of *homo sapiens christiana*, the local church congregation, as to be considered endangered species.

Endangered species

The International Union for Conservation of Nature (IUCN) is the global authority on the status of endangered species. Their 'Red List' includes 105,700 species, more than 28,000 of which are threatened with extinction.[10] Experts refer to the Red List as a 'Barometer of Life'. Just as a barometer measures atmospheric pressure and can be used to inform preparedness for adverse weather events, the Red List measures the pressures acting on species, with a view to shaping conservation policy and guiding actions to help prevent extinctions and reverse the decline in biodiversity.

In establishing its Rewilding Task Force, the IUCN has recognised the need to 'move beyond a simple structural bio-diversity approach to ecosystems and instead recognise the dynamic nature of the biodiversity of biological processes'. To put it more simply, they want to pursue actions that are more 'nature-led' or, in other words, promote rewilding.

Following the publication of *The Invisible Church* I was pleasantly surprised by the number of people who got in touch with a variety of feedback, questions, critique, thanks and requests. Leaders of church congregations asked for help in applying the insights to their particular situation. Christians who were not engaged with a local church congregation said that they felt less alone and had come to a better understanding of their own journey in faith and out of church. In addition, a few people who were involved in academic study and interested to compare notes or collaborate made contact. Among the latter, one message that particularly caught my attention was from Dawn Martindale, a person embarking on a dissertation related to how an understanding of personality characteristics might help in the development of discipleship, worship, and mission in the life of church congregations.

---

10 www.iucnredlist.org/.

Dawn and I kept in touch. I was impressed with the rigour of her studies, as she sought to better understand how people's personal characteristics influenced how they experienced some particular church congregations. She shared a copy of her final dissertation and, in a passing comment, suggested that it would be interesting to conduct some similar research among Christians who were not involved with traditional church congregations. The idea stuck with me and led to us collaborating to re-survey the churchless Christians I had surveyed five years earlier.

The survey comprised three parts. First we asked them about any experience of church congregations in the five years since we were last in touch. If they had re-engaged with a church congregation we were keen to hear more about that. Second, we asked them to complete a questionnaire called the Francis Psychological Types Scales (FPTS). This is a set of questions that would enable us to compile a profile of personality characteristics. Third, another questionnaire, the New Indices of Religious Orientation (NIRO), explored the nature of their Christian faith (more of that later). If that all sounds like gobbledegook, don't worry. All will be explained. And it's important.

Personality was something I had explored in *The Invisible Church*, but mainly based on the evidence of other people's studies. In study after study in church congregations across the Western world, some personality characteristics are consistently and significantly over-represented when compared to wider society, and others are underrepresented.

The main approach to researching personality that has been used to develop our understanding of dynamics within church congregations uses psychometric testing. Questionnaires are used to measure 'preferences' in different aspects of our psychology. A helpful comparison is with handedness. If we are left-handed, we will be perfectly able to use our right hand for some tasks, but will have a *preference* for using the left. For some people, whether in handedness or in the various aspects of psychology, a preference will be strong and for others it may be less so. So the tool we used, the FPTS, assesses the psychological preferences of people with regard to four pairs of opposites. For the sake of clarity I will explain all four pairs, but will focus on one of them in particular as highlighting a personality characteristic that is conspicuously absent from the congregational habitat.

The first pair of opposites is the spectrum of introvert-extrovert. People who prefer frequent interaction with others are likely to demonstrate through their responses to the questionnaire that they are somewhere on the extrovert side of the continuum; those whose responses show a tendency to replenish their energy through time alone will be on the introvert side of the scale. There is no right or wrong implied. Even people who have a strong preference can act in ways associated with the opposite type. However, their *natural inclination* is to act as might be expected from their psychological type. Through exploring psychological type scientists have discovered one of the many extraordinary ways in which we are each unique. As we better understand our psychological preferences, along with all the other amazing and delightful characteristics that make us who we are, we will find ourselves in harmony with the Hebrew poet who wrote, 'I praise you, for I am *fearfully and wonderfully made*'.[11]

The second continuum along which people have a natural preference relates to how they gather information from the world around them. We all exhibit a preference for either the details we collect through the five senses, or for the broader patterns and links we notice. Of course, we all gather information in both ways but some, described in psychology parlance as 'sensing' – those who focus on what comes from their five senses – tend to have a strong awareness of the present and their main attention is on the here and now; they are interested in details, facts and the practical. On the other side of this spectrum are those termed 'intuitive', people who tend to view the overall picture, giving greater attention to broad patterns rather than specific details.

One way of understanding psychological preference is to think of each preference as a different voice. We all hear all the

---

11 Psalm 139:14.

voices, but some voices are louder and clearer than others. So, for a 'sensing' person, when it comes to details the volume is high and each word well-defined, but the wider context with its general themes and patterns is quieter and perhaps a little muffled; for the 'intuitive' person, the overarching story or idea is loud and clear, but the details may be hazy.

Studies of psychological type in church congregations invariably show a strong over-representation of people with a preference for 'sensing' and a corresponding under-representation of 'intuitive' types. As explained in *The Invisible Church* when discussing the tendency for change-resistant cultures to develop in church congregations, this means that the typical congregation is dominated by people whose natural preference is for the conservative and conventional, those who tend to favour what is well-known, tried and tested, and well-established. 'Whereas intuitive types tend to be open to change and innovation, sensing types find the uncertainty and doubt involved to be distressing.'[12] Research shows that sensing types are inclined to view traditional expressions of Christianity more positively.[13]

Critically endangered thinkers

While our position on the sensing-intuitive continuum reveals how we prefer to *gather* information, the third scale is about how we then evaluate and apply that data. This is of particular interest because it highlights a rarity in the traditional Christian habitat of church congregations. So it is this third spectrum between 'thinking' and 'feeling' that I want to draw particular attention to. Of course, we all think and we all feel; the way these terms are used in psychology is unrelated to how well

---

12 Aisthorpe, S., 2016, *The Invisible Church: Learning from the Experiences of Churchless Christians*, Edinburgh, Saint Andrew Press, p. 118.

13 Francis, L. J. and C. F. J. Ross, 1997, 'The perceiving function and Christian spirituality: distinguishing between sensing and intuition', *Pastoral Sciences*, 16, pp. 173–91.

we do either. People who have a preference for 'thinking', as that term is used in psychological type theory, tend to be more objective and emphasise logic. Those with a tendency for 'feeling' give more importance to the subjective. The consistent finding of numerous studies across the Western world is that 'feeling' types are very common in church congregations and that, if there was a Red List for endangered species within church congregations, 'thinking' types would be listed as 'Critically Endangered'.

Finally, the fourth pair of preferences is termed 'judging-perceiving'. Those with a 'judging' type place high value on organisation and planning, whereas 'perceiving' types place greater importance on flexibility and spontaneity. In studies that have profiled the psychological preferences of churchgoers, most people show a preference for 'judging' rather than 'perceiving'. The perceiving types too are on the endangered list.

When the preferences that are least commonplace in church congregations are combined, they describe people who are almost extinct in terms of congregational life. So the chances of finding people who have preferences for intuition *and* thinking *and* perceiving in church congregations are minimal. The strong prevalence of the opposite types leads to ways of expressing faith and being community that are comfortable for those people, but demanding for others; dominant groups inadvertently create environments that favour their preferences and are challenging for others.

What my friend Dawn discovered in her study of four Baptist churches in Scotland[14] is remarkably similar to that found in similar research in England, Wales, Italy, Australia and the USA. While there are sixteen possible combinations of psychological type, it is generally agreed that four so-called 'temperaments' can be identified, based on four pairs of characteristics. One of these is the pairing of sensing and judging characteristics. Known as SJ, this temperament is incredibly common in

---

14 Martindale, D., 2018, 'Critically discuss the use of Psychological Type theory for the development of discipleship, worship, and mission in the life of a congregation', unpublished dissertation for the University of the Highlands and Islands, Highland Theological College.

church congregations. In Dawn's study 76.3 per cent were SJ and, while this is the most common temperament in the UK as a whole (49 per cent), this substantial over-representation in church congregations is verified by numerous studies. While the profiles that are especially rare in church congregations are some of the smallest groups in society as a whole, their rarity in churches is considerably more pronounced.

The number of churchless Christians Dawn and I were able to survey was small, so we need to be cautious about drawing general conclusions. However, it was striking that many of these churchless Christians could be described as species that are rare in church congregations. For example, 40 per cent showed preference for 'thinking', fitting with the findings of a study with a much larger sample. In Matthew Baker's study of 'Psychological type differences between churchgoers and church-leavers', all of the types most significantly over-represented among the church-leavers included a preference for thinking.[15] What are we to make of this?

While people are generally blind to the kinds of differences measured by psychometric tests, there is now an abundance of evidence to show that they make important and tangible differences to how people engage with various aspects of the Christian faith and community. For example, in the latest of a series of similar studies, researchers worked with a group of Anglican clergy and trainees on a residential programme. They were split into groups according to whether they were 'sensing' or 'intuitive' in terms of psychological type. All were invited to read the same passage of Scripture and consider what they understood from the teaching of Jesus on the lost sheep. As might be predicted, sensing types 'focused on important details', while intuitive types 'allowed the passage to spark multiple ideas'.[16]

---

15 Baker, M., 2015, 'Psychological type differences between church-goers and church-leavers', *Mental Health, Religion & Culture*, 18(7), pp. 622–34.

16 Francis, L. and S. Jones, 2019, 'Searching for the Lost Sheep (Matthew 18:10–14): Do sensing types and intuitive types find different things', *Rural Theology*, 17(2), p. 106.

Those who have studied the kinds of habitat in which 'thinkers' thrive report that they need an environment that offers intellectual stretching, welcomes logic and encourages questioning.[17] Those who have investigated the prayer lives of people with diverse psychological preferences observe that those with a 'thinking' preference favour an approach to God that is rational and intellectual and are likely to struggle with acts of corporate worship and teaching planned and delivered by people with a strong 'feeling' preference.[18] Whereas the majority in church congregations who have a preference for 'feeling' find prayer and worship to be emotional activities, for the critically endangered 'thinkers', spirituality has a strong cerebral element and the act of consciously thinking can be prayer.

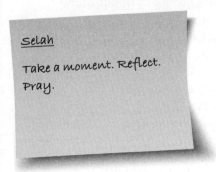

Selah

Take a moment. Reflect. Pray.

Where the endangered thrive

If the white tailed eagle is the most majestic of our native birds, a strong contender for the most elegant must be the avocet. With their stylish pied plumage and slender blue legs, troupes of these nimble waders can give the impression of performing a carefully choreographed ballet. Breeding around shallow muddy pools where they sweep their slender up-turned bills back and forth to catch tiny crustaceans and worms, how they maintain such an impeccable appearance is a mystery. Ancient records show that these attractive waders were numerous along the east coast of England until, in the 1820s, probably due to the collecting of eggs and specimens, they became extinct as a breeding species for more than a century. The tale of their

17 Goldsmith, M., 1997, *Knowing Me Knowing God*, Nashville, TN: Abingdon Press, pp. 78–9.
18 Duncan, B., 1994, *Pray Your Way: Personality and God*, London: Darton, Longman and Todd.

return is a lesson in the foundational premise of rewilding, the ability of nature to bounce back when given a chance. Although their now healthy population is often credited to conservation efforts, their initial return was almost certainly an unintended consequence of radical and unplanned changes to land use. The dates of their comeback provide clues as to why the lagoons and mudflats of these eastern counties once again became desirable residences for these long-absent waders. They first reappeared in the early 1940s. They bred in Norfolk in 1941, then in Essex in 1944 and Suffolk was recolonised in 1947.

We have already noted that some of the most dramatic examples of rewilding have been the inadvertent outcomes of conflict or humanitarian crises and in this case it was the Second World War. As coastal areas were closed to the public and flooded as a defence against invasion, a habitat of the shallow scrapes and undisturbed lagoons that constitute avocet heaven re-emerged.[19] While it would be wrong to credit conservation organisations with the initial return of this iconic bird, they should certainly be congratulated for learning from what happened and applying to other areas the insights gained from observing accidental success stories.

If reflecting on the inadvertent reintroduction of the avocet provided the wisdom for their colonisation to be extended, where might we look in the Church to find endangered species finding hospitable habitat and gaining a foothold in Christian community? This is a valuable question to ask in any local context and the findings of research provide some clear pointers as to where to look. Studies of cathedrals, fresh expressions of Church, Greek Orthodox congregations and churchless Christians all provide evidence that forms of Christian community that are substantially different to conventional church congregations provide habitats for some of the endangered species we have identified. The data also suggests that characteristics such as gender, psychological type or religious

---

19 Davis, S., 2011, 'Militarised natural history: tales of the avocet's return to postwar Britain', *Studies in History and Philosophy of Science Part C: Studies in History and Philosophy of Biological and Biomedical Science*, June 42(2), pp. 226–32.

orientation (see below) are interrelated and that unless we get beyond superficial observations and shallow assumptions, we are likely to draw conclusions that are, at best, simplistic or, worse, misguided.

Take gender for example. Being easy to detect, observations about a lack of men in church congregations are common-place, but diagnoses of a 'feminisation' of church cultures and prescriptions for congregational life to appeal more to adventure-loving males are often based more on anecdote and stereotypes than evidence.[20] The role of gender in the decline of congregational Christianity in the UK is complex and more to do with changing understandings of gender than alterations in church culture.[21] What empirical evidence *does* show is that church contexts where men are more prevalent seem to cater well for the thinking types that have become so rare in conventional congregations. Research in cathedrals and Greek Orthodox congregations, both of which tend to have higher proportions of men than the wider churchgoing popu-lation, reveals a preponderance of thinking types, including among the women of those congregations. A study in South-wark Cathedral found that nearly 60 per cent of men were the endangered thinking type.[22] Data from Greek Orthodox congregations found more than two-thirds of male attendees to be thinkers.[23] Research that compared the psychological

---

20 The former is a central tenet in Murrow, D., 2005, *Why Men Hate Going to Church*, Nashville, TN: Thomas Nelson; the latter is argued in Eldridge, J., 2010, *Wild at Heart – Discovering the Secret of a Man's Soul*, Nashville, TN: Thomas Nelson.

21 Scottish historian Callum Brown has explored in detail how changes in sexual practices and gendered roles have impacted on church attendance. Brown, C., 2009, *The Death of Christian Britain: Under-standing Secularisation, 1800–2000*, Abingdon: Routledge; Brown, C., 2010, 'Sex, religion and the single woman c.1950–1975: the impor-tance of a "short" sexual revolution to the English religious crisis of the sixties', *Twentieth-Century British History*, 22(2), pp. 189–215.

22 Francis, L. J. and David W. Lankshear, 2015, 'Inside Southwark Cathedral: a study in the congregation's motivational style', *Journal of Beliefs & Values*, 36(3), pp. 276–84.

23 Lewis, C. A., G. Varvatsoulias and E. Williams, 2012, 'The psy-

types of people from a large sample of Anglican churchgoers with those of people engaged with fresh expressions of Church found significant differences, including the relative prevalence of some of the endangered species we have mentioned.[24] Fresh expressions tend to have an intentional focus on particular groups of people, but these are usually defined in terms of social categories such as generation, interest groups, housing or stage of life. However, in pioneering new manifestations of Church, they appear to be inadvertently providing environments in which certain psychological types can thrive. In stark contrast to the preponderance of sensing and feeling types in church congregations in general, the data from fresh expressions showed that most men demonstrated a strong preference for intuition (65 per cent) over sensing (35 per cent), for thinking (63 per cent) over feeling (37 per cent) and for judging (74 per cent) over perceiving (26 per cent). Among women too, while only 19 per cent of those engaged in conventional congregations showed a preference for intuition, that proportion was 35 per cent in fresh expressions.

Christian young adults are another species that is absent from many church congregations. A minority subset – those who are well educated, from middle-class backgrounds and who previously attended church as children – are well represented in some large congregations, but even these are absent from many smaller congregations. However, in her research in fresh expressions of Church, Beth Keith found other young adults prospering, including those with no prior faith or church experience and from a broad socio-economic background.[25] The habitats in which these thriving pockets of young adults were found were characterised by cultures where 'value was placed

---

chological type profile of practicing Greek Orthodox churchgoers in London', *Mental Health, Religion & Culture*, 15(10), pp. 983–4.

24 Francis, L. J., J. Clymo and M. Robbins, 2014, 'Fresh expressions: reaching those psychological types conventional forms of church find it hard to reach?', *Practical Theology*, 7(4), pp. 252–67.

25 Keith, B., 2013, *Authentic Faith: Fresh Expressions of Church amongst Young Adults*, Sheffield, Fresh Expressions.

on an openness to express doubt, to question, to deconstruct'.[26] These young adults described their experience of Church in terms of 'journeying together, working out faith, together, in the messy realities of life, rather than the teaching of truths'.[27]

The RSPB may not be able to claim responsibility for reintroducing the avocet to the UK, but they certainly took note of what unintentionally happened and used the learning to create habitats for the recolonization that ensued. As followers of Jesus with a concern for the thriving of the kingdom and the Church, we should note that the rich diversity of humankind needs a miscellany of opportunities for Christian fellowship, nurture and worship. Monoculture in expressions of Church leads to the thriving of some species and the dramatic declines of others. Cathedrals, Greek Orthodox congregations and fresh expressions of Church make up a minority of church-going in the UK, but they are demonstrating the benefits of ecclesiastical biodiversity.

Same reintroduction, different reasons

In November 2016 it was announced that a species that would have certainly been on the Red List in the past was, once again, officially designated as a native British species. The size and weight of an average Labrador, the reappearance of Eurasian Beavers in UK rivers is causing a splash. Prior to recent reintroductions, the last reference to this influential species in England dates back to 1526 and it seems likely that they had become extinct in the whole of the UK by the end of the sixteenth century. With luxuriant fur, delicious meat and a secretion from its scent gland believed to have medicinal properties, Eurasian Beavers were hunted vigorously. By the beginning of the twentieth century they clung on in just eight remnant pockets across Europe and Asia.

The recent reintroduction was undertaken with caution. As multiple generations of UK inhabitants have only encountered

---

26 Keith, *Authentic Faith*, p. 12.
27 Keith, *Authentic Faith*, p. 12.

this second largest rodent in the world through stereotypical depictions in children's literature and films, it is unsurprising that opinions about their reinstatement have been mixed. Only after considerable consultation, and the careful perusal of similar programmes in other countries, was a small trial allowed. Then between May 2009 and September 2010 sixteen beavers in four family groups were introduced to three lochs in the Knapdale Forest of Argyll. By May 2014 *The Guardian* reported that 'The four pairs of beavers ... have produced 14 young, engineered 18-metre-long dams and lodges the size of double garages and significantly boosted tourism.'[28] Examining the environmental impact of the beavers on biodiversity, forestry and hydrology, researchers found that the animals had transformed the landscape, constructing dams, felling trees, creating canals and building lodges. By making space for this long-absent species, the environment was being changed for *all* its inhabitants and while most have judged the return of these rodents 'an outstanding success', the changes that are being wrought create challenges for some. While they are now officially 'native species', their population and impacts are being carefully monitored, lessons are being learned and the people most impacted by their arrival carefully consulted.

One striking fact in reviewing the story of the beaver's homecoming is that people have advocated for their return for distinctly different reasons. For some people, the primary argument for returning a species that was previously excluded by the actions of humankind was a moral one: we are guilty of persecuting their ancestors, so doing all we can to right that previous wrong is the proper and just course of action. For others, the hoped-for benefits of these creatures on the wider environment was the compelling reason for making space for them in a landscape that has been without them for centuries. For such people, there was a pragmatic, utilitarian case for bringing back a population of animals who can help

---

28 Aldred, J., 2014, 'Scotland wild beaver reintroduction trial "an outstanding success"', 14 May, *The Guardian*, www.theguardian.com/environment/2014/may/14/scotland-wild-beaver-reintroduced-knapdale (accessed 26.11.2019).

to solve environmental problems. Evidence from other areas demonstrating how the presence of beavers helps to reduce downstream flooding convinced many, regardless of where they stood on the moral debate, that they were a valuable and welcome arrival. A third lobby for the reintroduction of this species reasoned from the perspective of the expected benefits for the local ecosystems, the river systems in which they would reside. Regardless of possible benefits in flood relief or economic paybacks through eco-tourism, beavers were hailed by some people as creators of richer and more diverse wetlands through their carving of canal systems and coppicing tree and shrub species. Those who made this argument may or may not have embraced the moral case and saw the wider hydrological or economic benefits in different ways, but for them greater biodiversity and the benefits to other species, such as shrews, voles, invertebrates, fish and birds, were sufficient grounds for bringing back these 'ecosystem engineers'.

These three distinct perspectives have brought together activists from a variety of sectors for a shared purpose. Ecologists, farmers, tourism development organisations and environmental engineers may have different reasons for wanting the beavers to thrive, but their collaboration has led to the establishment of a sustainable population of this long-extinct mammal. Particular individuals may have strong moral, utilitarian and ecological opinions or their concerns may be in just one or two of these areas, but together a partnership has developed with the clear and common goal that beavers should thrive again.

Earlier in this chapter I mentioned that when the cohort of churchless Christians from the 2013 *Investigating the Invisible Church* research were re-surveyed five years later, in addition to exploring psychological type we also used a survey tool called the New Indices of Religious Orientation (NIRO) to better understand the nature of their Christian faith. The concept of 'religious orientation' has had a major impact on the psychology of religion in recent decades. Beginning with the ground-breaking work of Gordon Allport in the 1960s,[29] psy-

---

29 Allport, G., 1966, 'Religious context of prejudice', *Journal of the Scientific Study of Religion*, Autumn 5(3), p. 5.

chologists began to recognise and understand that the essence of people's religious faith could be seen as having intrinsic or extrinsic orientations. Intrinsic orientation 'regards faith as a supreme value in its own right ... A religious sentiment of this sort floods the whole life with motivations and meanings.'[30] The original *Investigating the Invisible Church* research found that about half of a large random sample of people who identified themselves as Christians but not regular churchgoers were high scorers on a scale of this intrinsic religious orientation.[31] 'High scores on this [intrinsic] scale indicate that a person's faith underpins all that they do; their faith is core to their motivation and, in this sense, they live their faith.'[32]

People with a strong *extrinsic* religious orientation are motivated by the 'usefulness' of their faith. 'Persons with this orientation may find religion useful ... to provide security and solace, sociability and distraction, status and self-justification.'[33] Psychologists who continued to develop this line of enquiry through the 1970s and 1980s found that to more fully understand the motivations of religious faith it was important to assess a third orientation. This is what has been dubbed 'quest orientation'. 'The quest orientation gave recognition to a form of religiosity which embraces characteristics of complexity, doubt, tentativeness, and honesty in facing existential questions.'[34] For a person with a strong quest orientation, exploring questions that are thrown up by their experience of the world is at the heart of their faith. These people 'display openness to change and a readiness to embrace new perspectives. They freely admit that there are many religious issues on which their

30 Allport, 'Religious context of prejudice', p. 455.

31 Aisthorpe, S., 2016, *The Invisible Church: Learning from the Experiences of Churchless Christians*, Edinburgh: Saint Andrew Press, p. 54.

32 Aisthorpe, *Invisible Church*, p. 53.

33 Allport, G. and J. Ross, 1967, 'Personal religious orientation and prejudice', *Journal of Personality and Social Psychology*, 5, p. 434.

34 Francis, L., 2007, 'Introducing the New Indices of Religious Orientation (NIRO): conceptualization and measurement', *Mental Health, Religion & Culture*, 10(6), p. 588.

views are still changing.'[35] Doubt is seen by those with a strong quest orientation in a positive way and is understood as being fundamental to faith. While the world of beaver reintroduction programmes and religious faith are fundamentally different, the complex motivations of people in both spheres display different orientations or perspectives.

Same faith, three 'orientations'

In considering religious orientation it is vital to realise that an individual is not *either* one orientation *or* another. It would be an abuse of this kind of psychological tool to assign one orientation to a person. We all have elements of intrinsic, extrinsic and quest orientation. One orientation may be dominant, but even then there will still be indications of the others at work. In fact, what a substantial body of empirical evidence shows is that 'How you score on one component says precisely nothing about how you will score on the other two. The three are independent dimensions.'[36] A passionate advocate for the reintroduction of beavers may be motivated primarily by moral arguments, but may also be inspired and encouraged by the case for local and wider benefits, both for humankind and other species. With religious orientation, assuming a person has a religious faith, they might score high on all three components, or high on one or two and low on another.

What our modest study of Christians in Scotland who are not engaged with a local congregation reveals is that for 40 per cent of those people quest orientation is their dominant component. These are people for whom asking questions and exploring doubts is not only important, it is fundamental to their faith. In *The Invisible Church* I offered a simple generalised model of disengagement from congregational life. Based

---

35 Francis, 'Introducing the New Indices of Religious Orientation', p. 598.
36 Batson, C., P. Schoerade and W. Ventis, 1993, *Religion and the Individual: A Social-Psychological Perspective*, New York, NY: Oxford University Press, p. 174.

on the experiences of hundreds of church-leavers we listened to and surveyed, the 'road to post-congregational faith' has as its first stage 'Asking questions and exploring doubts'.[37] The data gathered since then reinforces and highlights the insight that lack of opportunities to do that leads to the next stage, 'cumulative disaffection'. An understanding of quest religious orientation explains why such a dynamic would occur. When a person's faith is exercised and developed by questioning, but that is frustrated or actively discouraged, mounting frustration is inevitable. Other studies, from England and Wales[38] to Australia,[39] 'point to the problems that some people have found in locating churches in which a quest approach to faith is acceptable'.[40] While the values and attitudes typified in those who are high scorers on quest orientation find plenty of echoes in the pages of the Scriptures, it seems that these are not encouraged in the habitats of many church congregations. Providing a welcoming environment to beavers has not only led to them becoming established; their mosaics of dams, pools and wetlands are providing new homes for an array of native wildlife, dragonflies and frogs, water birds and otters – the benefits cascade through the ecosystem. Fostering Christian cultures with healthy attitudes to questions and doubts is vital for those with strong quest orientation, but the benefits will not stop there. Just as the presence of some species creates habitats for others to thrive, the presence of those psychological types and religious orientations that are often missing from church

37 Aisthorpe, S., 2016, *The Invisible Church: Learning from the Experiences of Churchless Christians*, Edinburgh: Saint Andrew Press, pp. 65–77.

38 Richter, P. and L. J. Francis, 1998, *Gone but Not Forgotten: Churchleaving and Returning*, London: Darton, Longman & Todd; Francis, L. J. and P. Richter, 2007, *Gone for Good?: Church-leaving and Returning in the 21st Century*, Peterborough: Epworth Press.

39 Francis, L., A. Village and R. Powell, 2016, 'Religious experience and religious motivation among Catholic and mainstream Protestant churchgoers in Australia: testing and applying five short measures', *Mental Health, Religion & Culture*, 19(8), https://ray.yorksj.ac.uk/id/eprint/2127/1/VillageReligious%20experience%20and%20religious%20motivation%20ACCEPTED.pdf, pp. 932–42.

40 Francis, Village and Powell, 'Religious experience', p. 14.

congregations will enrich the environment for everyone when connections are made.

A recent Moderator of the Church of Scotland explained in an interview that he had been banned from Sunday School as a seven-year-old for being 'a disruptive influence'. His crime, apparently, was 'asking too many questions'! Some Christians with a strong quest orientation find relationships and institutions in which they thrive, but interviews with people who have disengaged from congregational life are littered with experiences of congregations and groups that provide environments hostile to those who 'ask too many questions'. 'When eager disciples cannot find in church the space and companionship they need to explore questions and doubts, they seek these things elsewhere.'[41] Creating environments where asking questions and exploring doubts are positively encouraged is not only about saving an endangered species by creating a habitat for those of strong quest orientation. Even congregations and groups who have experimented with discussion-based formats in a limited way through courses such as Alpha, Emmaus and similar resources report benefits beyond the course itself, as the asking of questions and voicing of doubts becomes more acceptable.

One flock, many habitats

The observant reader of the Gospels will notice that while both Luke and Matthew record a parable about a diligent shepherd seeking out a single lost sheep,[42] the emphasis of the two is different. In Luke's account it is set alongside the parables of the lost sons and the lost coin. The emphasis is on the Son of Man's desire and determination to bring home lost people. Its purpose is evangelistic. In Matthew, a similar parable has a different function. As one New Testament scholar puts it, 'The purpose here is clearly pastoral.'[43] Like so many of the

41 Aisthorpe, *The Invisible Church*, p. 68.
42 Matthew 18:10–14; Luke 15:3–7.
43 Green, M., 2000, *The Message of Matthew*, London: IVP, p. 193.

parables of Jesus, the impact and meaning is easily lost on contemporary Western ears. People used to seeing sheep kept in large flocks and herded by dogs or quadbikes easily miss some of the connections Jesus expected his hearers to make when they heard the word 'shepherd'. The shepherds of ancient Palestine kept relatively small flocks, harvesting their wool over several years. They really did *know* their sheep. Flocks were often communally owned and shepherded, making it possible for sheep to be left in safe hands while one shepherd sought out an individual. Matthew sets this parable in the context of teaching on relationships in the kingdom, where so many of the world's values and priorities are turned on their head. Jesus is instructing the prospective leaders of his Church on the vital importance of looking out for the ones who are missing. No 'little ones' are to be disregarded or neglected; God's unrelenting, compassionate, seeking love calls for us to look around, to notice who is missing and to recognise that they too are part of the one flock.

I am certainly not suggesting that anyone should chase after people with the intention of corralling them into homogenised congregations! An important aspect of God's rewilding of the Church is reflected in the emergence of many small groups of pilgriming friends, creating habitats where those unable to thrive in traditional congregations can flourish. However, the Church will be enriched when we notice our differences, celebrate our diversity and build connections of mutual learning and sharing.

Selah

Pause. Consider. Pray.

8

CONNECT: Growing Relationships

'Next to them Uzziel son of Harhaiah, one of the
   goldsmiths, made repairs.
Next to him Hananiah, one of the perfumers, made repairs;
   and they restored
Jerusalem as far as the Broad Wall. Next to them Rephaiah
   son of Hur,
ruler of half the district of Jerusalem, made repairs.'
                                          Nehemiah 3:8–9

Okay, admit it – did you actually read the names in the verses
from Nehemiah printed above or did you just skip over them?
At first glance the third chapter of Nehemiah is not the most
inspiring passage in the Bible. It is, on one level at least, a long
list of names. And what names! There are Eliashib, Zaccur son
of Imri, the sons of Hassenaah, Meremoth son of Uriah son of
Hakkoz, Meshullam son of Berechiah son of Meshezabel ...
and that is just the beginning. Some of the people named here
make an appearance elsewhere in our Scriptures, but many
do not. On the whole they are utterly unknown to us. Like
the war memorials that stand at the heart of so many British
villages, here is an extensive inventory of names, most of which
mean little or nothing to us. However, like those names on
monuments and cenotaphs, as we read the names we know
that they were people like us, that they were loved by someone,
certainly loved by God, and that they participated in something colossal. In most cases their individual part was minor,
but, joining with myriad others, they had an immense impact;
they contributed something to a gigantic undertaking.
   It would have been easy for Nehemiah to leave us with an
impersonal project report, simply detailing what was achieved

in what timescale and with what resources. The fact that what we have instead is a record of people, partnerships and attitudes says a great deal. Thirty-eight people are mentioned by name. We are told that they came from a variety of places:˙ Jericho, Tekoa, Gibeon, Mizpah, Zelah. Their backgrounds and skills were miscellaneous to say the least. Some were obvious choices for a challenging building assignment in the face of armed oppression; others less clearly so. Within the team there were goldsmiths, priests, guards, merchants, servants, rulers, Levites and at least one perfume maker. No doubt their personalities and temperaments were similarly assorted, bringing all the usual interpersonal challenges of any shared endeavour. Archaeologists have been amazed by the extent and quality of what was achieved by this extraordinary partnership. In fifty-two days an encircling wall some two and a half metres thick, complete with massive, secure gates and multiple towers, was completed.[1]

Further reflection reveals that, far from being a humdrum list of players, this is an account of an exemplary collaboration. There are only thirty-two verses in this third chapter of Nehemiah, and yet within this catalogue of names the phrase 'next to him' or 'next to them' occurs twenty-six times. Despite their many differences, these people worked together with outstanding effectiveness. Forty-two sections of wall are recorded and most of the people mentioned focused on one part of the overall undertaking. However, for the end result to be a single, coherent and reliable structure required meticulous coordination and consistent collaboration. It was not sufficient for each part of the wall to abut the neighbouring sections. A fragmented collection of individual building projects, even if their build quality was exceptional, would just not do. The strength of this vital defensive construction required wholehearted commitment to the same shared vision; structural integrity was the result of human connection.

When preaching on Nehemiah recently I reminded the congregation of the story that is told about another astonishing

---

1 Mazar, Eilat, 2009, 'The wall that Nehemiah built', *Biblical Archaeology Review*, Mar/Apr.

building project. The year was 1678 and the setting was the City of London. Work on what was to become St Paul's Cathedral was still in its early stages and, unknown to the workforce, the building's brilliant designer, Christopher Wren, was visiting the site. He moved among the throng of industrious stone cutters, engineers and carpenters, casting a careful eye over proceedings and enquiring about the activities of various workers. One mason, asked about the task at hand, replied, 'I'm cutting this block of stone'. Coming to another craftsman, apparently engaged in a similar activity, Wren enquired again. This time the answer was different: 'I'm trying to put some bread on the table for my family'. The incognito architect continued his tour and asked the same question of a third worker, 'What are you doing?' He too was cutting and shaping a hefty slab of Portland limestone. With a glint in his eye, he straightened his back and exclaimed, 'I'm building a great cathedral for my God.' Whether actual, apocryphal or just adapted through the centuries, I have no idea, but it is a powerful anecdote regardless.

Like Uzziel son of Harhaiah, Hananiah, the creator of fine fragrances, and each of the diverse band of workhands that comprised 'Team Nehemiah' – and like the artisans, engineers and labourers whose combined commitment, skills and efforts created the iconic Baroque masterpiece of St Paul's – we have a role in a magnificent and worthwhile undertaking. We are commissioned to participate in the most momentous enterprise ever, a scheme of ultimate significance and eternal consequence. The architect and the one who will see the project through to its flawless completion, its author and perfecter, is none other than Jesus Christ.

Some crucial challenges confront us. The first is to again and again and again refocus our attention on Jesus and the vision he imparted, the kingdom, his certain intention to redeem all of creation and to restore his seamless reign. As I have reflected elsewhere, a failure to keep the King and his kingdom front and centre is at the root of much individual and congregational malaise:

Without regular refocusing ... congregations tend to degenerate from being a movement to being a monument, from being dynamic to being static. Eagerness to follow and serve and grow in Christ gives way to routine, monotony and boredom. What was a genuine adventure of faith becomes predictable, humdrum and dreary ... Dedication to living out the Christian faith and loyal maintenance of the institution become intertwined and muddled. Having moved from 'movement to monument', the next stage is 'mausoleum'.[2]

A second challenge is to discern and faithfully fulfil our unique and vital contribution, a matter explored further in Chapter 5. A third task, the focus of this chapter, is to cultivate the kind of connections that create the profound and powerful partnership we long for, connections rooted in relationships of remarkable quality.

Rewilding in the ecological sphere is demonstrating the disproportionate power of connections. Linking small territories to create a larger habitat often leads to impacts out of all proportion to the linkages involved. With the emphasis Jesus put on the importance of conserving our connection with him, 'the vine'[3] and Paul's imagery of the Church as 'the body of Christ',[4] it is unsurprising that the rewilding of the Church demands attention to our connections of multiple kinds. In Chapter 4 we looked at reconnecting with the source, with Jesus himself; here we explore connections with one another, with the great traditions that are the Church's streams of life, and with wider society.

---

2 Aisthorpe, S., 2016, *The Invisible Church: Learning from the Experiences of Churchless Christians*, Edinburgh: Saint Andrew Press, pp. 113–14.

3 John 15:1–8.

4 1 Corinthians 12:12–27.

The wood wide web

In recent years scientists have discovered that what some indigenous peoples have believed for millennia is true. The suspicions of people who have spent their lifetime watching nature are now backed up by scientific data. When the late John Muir[5] suggested that, 'When we try to pick out anything by itself, we find it hitched to everything else in the Universe',[6] it was an idea based on a lifetime of intimate observation, but lacked scientific data. He would laugh and derive immense satisfaction from the research findings of biologists that now demonstrate the ways in which trees communicate and interact.

We've always known that the root systems of trees can be huge, often extending over more than double the area of their crown. We've known for a long time that some species are bound together in a single root system. Close to my home is a group of aspen trees. As they only flower and reproduce by wind pollination after an exceptionally warm summer, and because this is the Highlands of Scotland we're talking about, this year was the first time they had flowered for twenty-three years! When, in normal summer temperatures, they are unable to produce their exquisite pink catkins, they need to find other ways to reproduce and do so by sending up suckers from their roots, which then grow into trees. From our viewpoint, above ground, they are individual trees. What appears as woodland comprised of multiple trees is in fact, genetically, one. As I enjoy the exquisite tinselly trembling of their leaves, I am reminded that while the array of church congregations is as diverse as it is vast, they, along with the multitudes of Christians whose fellowship is largely non-congregational, comprise one Church.

Let's dig a little deeper – into the forest floor – and what recent discoveries have to show us about life down there. When

---

5 John Muir was a Scottish emigrant to the United States, where he is credited as 'father of the National Parks' and was an early environmental activist.

6 Muir, J., 1988, *My First Summer in the Sierra*, San Francisco: CA: Sierra Club, p. 110.

we stand in woodland, beneath our feet are immeasurable networks of fine, thread-like filaments of fungi known as 'hyphae'. The extent and complexity of these systems are incalculable, as is their value to the plants they connect. Through these vast fungal grids, signals are transmitted, warning of insect attacks, drought and other dangers. Trees and plants facing difficulties receive assistance from others. 'No plant is an island', as the journal *Nature Plants*[7] reported recently. Yes, trees really do talk to one another.[8]

Peter Wohlleben, who has made these ground-breaking scientific discoveries accessible to a wider readership through his unlikely bestseller *The Hidden Life of Trees*, describes what amounts to an intricate social security system, extending over huge distances and stretching through protracted episodes of time: 'One teaspoon of forest soil contains many miles of these "hyphae". Over centuries, a single fungus can cover many square miles and network an entire forest.'[9] Just read that sentence again. It's absolutely astounding.

As this previously unknown phenomenon came to light in the era of information technology, these fungal networks have been dubbed the 'wood wide web' and hyphae filaments have been likened to fibre optic cables. Imagine, however, if these discoveries had been made in the era of the early Church and first-century scientists were scouting around for metaphors or similes to illustrate their findings. The word used for the community that emerged from the events around Pentecost, *koinonia*, would have served them well. Luke's eyewitness account of *koinonia* in the Acts of the Apostles describes a network of radical participation, intimate communion and deep sharing. If, instead of alluding to the worldwide web, our imaginary first-century scientists chose *koinonia* to explain the astounding interconnections and mutuality they had unearthed,

7 'No plant is an island', *Nature Plants*, 2, 16146 (2016).

8 BBC News, 2018, 'How trees secretly talk to each other', 28 June, www.bbc.co.uk/news/av/science-environment-44643177/how-trees-secretly-talk-to-each-other (accessed 08.01.2020).

9 Wohlleben, P., 2016, *The Hidden Life of Trees*, London: Collins, p. 10.

they might also use *agape* instead of 'fibre optic cables' as a simile for what actually holds the network together.

'God is *agape*'[10] we are told in one of the Apostle John's letters; 'Just as I have loved you, you also should love one another',[11] Jesus instructed his followers. *Agape* is the kind of love that takes purposeful delight in the objects of that love, seeks the best for the other and exhibits the kind of enduring faithfulness, persistent patience and self-giving generosity that we read about in Paul's letter to the Corinthians.[12] The inventory of the 'fruit of the Spirit' actually comprises examples of this love in action. 'Joy is love exulting, and peace is love at rest; Patience, love enduring in every trial and test ...' go the opening lines of Kenneth Moynagh's poem. And it ends with the insightful conclusion, 'For Christ is love in person, and love, Christ in the soul.'[13]

Towards the end of his life, probably the only survivor of the original apostolic group at the time, when considering what few words to share with a fragile fledgling Christian community, John chose to highlight once again that this kind of love is the hallmark of healthy Christian relationships and the touchstone of authentic Christian fellowship: 'I am writing to remind you, dear friends, that we should love one another.'[14] A rewilded Church is characterised by *agape*-connected community.

Many of us long for loving community, but Dietrich Bonhoeffer warned of the danger of putting cart before horse and points to a better way. 'The person who loves their dream of community will destroy community. The person who loves those around them will create community.'[15] Research among fresh expressions of Church across the UK shows the truth of Bonhoeffer's words. A 'worship first' methodology to

---

10 1 John 4:8.

11 John 13:34.

12 1 Corinthians 13.

13 Dr Kenneth Moynagh was a medical missionary in Burundi and his poem is quoted in Stott, J., 1992, *The Contemporary Christian*, London: IVP, p. 156.

14 2 John 5 (NLT).

15 Bonhoeffer, D., 1954, *Life Together*, London: SCM Press.

church planting, where a viable group from a larger congregation begins a new congregation elsewhere, tends to create a congregation comprised largely of people relocated from other congregations; 'love first' approaches, where prayerful listening and sharing the love and wisdom of Jesus takes place in the context of an emerging community, are more likely to lead to communities rich in people who are new to Christian faith.[16]

Bodily connections

One of the most incredible and inspiring truths of the Christian faith is that the instant we accept the compelling invitation of Jesus, 'Follow me', we are connected to uncountable brothers and sisters, globally and throughout history. Our journey of following and listening and growing is not a lonely individual pilgrimage. If we ever imagined that travelling with Jesus was going to be a private one-on-one affair, we were seriously misguided. Jesus, we soon discover, is not only *my* gracious saviour, *my* guide, *my* exacting yet gracious Lord. As well as being the source of comprehensive forgiveness, ultimate authority, compelling inspiration and much, much more for *me*, he is also the wellspring of the very same for the entire family.

St Paul, once vehemently opposed to the way of Jesus and violently hostile to his early followers, was so awestruck, so utterly overwhelmed by this truth that, as he later wrote to fledgling churches far and wide, it seemed that no cascade of words could adequately express the profundity and implications of what Christ had made possible and what he had brought into being in what we call the Church. Reflecting on Paul's recurring use of the word 'lavish' – some forty-five times in his New Testament epistles – Eugene Peterson wonders whether he overdoes it a bit, but on reflection concludes that,

---

16 Lings, G., 2016, *The Day of Small Things: An Analysis of Fresh Expressions of Church in 21 Dioceses of the Church of England*, Church Army, pp. 43–6; Moynagh, M., 2017, *Church in Life: Innovation, Mission and Ecclesiology*, London: SCM Press, p. 45.

'In matters of God's grace, hyperboles are underestimates.'[17] As Paul heaps such language upon his readers, one senses that his torrent of extravagant vocabulary reaches a crescendo when he articulates in simple and organic terminology the indestructible connections that have been established between Christ and his followers and between these disciples themselves. Through the life, death and resurrection of Jesus, a 'body' had come into being which is the natural and organic extension of himself: body and head, intimately connected, working together, a common purpose and destiny.

'Jesus Christ ... conceived by the Holy Spirit ... born of the virgin Mary ... suffered under Pontius Pilate', the Apostles' Creed reminds us. The Church, the 'body of Christ', was born of the same Spirit at Pentecost into a remarkably similar context, a situation also characterised by physical vulnerability, religious marginalisation and political peril. With unbridled passion, Paul enthuses about the privilege and wonder of inclusion and participation in this community initiated, led and animated by Christ himself: 'All of you together are Christ's body, and each of you is a part of it.'[18] He celebrates the essential interconnectedness and inherent mutuality of Jesus' followers: 'We are many parts of one body, and we all belong to each other.'[19] He reminds his readers that God has lavished (that word again) gifts on his people for a purpose: 'to equip God's people to do his work and build up the church, the body of Christ'.[20] And he assures them that the ultimate outcome is inevitable: 'This will continue until we all come to such unity in our faith and knowledge of God's Son that we will be mature in the Lord, measuring up to the full and complete standard of Christ.'[21]

It is impossible to trump the high view of the Church espoused by the writers of the New Testament in general and

17 Peterson, E., 2010, *Practice Resurrection*, Colorado Springs, CO: Eerdmans, p. 63.

18 1 Corinthians 12:27 (NLT).

19 Romans 12:5 (NLT).

20 Ephesians 4:12 (NLT).

21 Ephesians 4:13 (NLT).

by Paul in particular. And yet, with predictable consistency, the same epistles that convey a glorious vision of Church go on to challenge and address the multiple ways in which the lived experiences of those first Christian communities consistently failed to reflect the character of Jesus. The canon of Scripture presents us with no perfect examples. No success stories are heralded. No role models are offered except for Jesus himself. The intimate and unbreakable connections between Christ and his body and between the innumerable members of that body are theological facts, but this side of eternity the existential reality is always incomplete, frequently distorted, occasionally toxic, sometimes glorious, and continuously in progress. Sometimes a source of inspiration, sometimes a cause for concern, at times nourishing us, at times draining us, ceaselessly changing us ... the unchosen connections between believers need our careful attention if we are concerned for the rewilding of the Church.

One of the most striking commonalities in the many accounts of people I have listened to throughout the 'invisible church' research projects is that when people disengage from a church congregation they have been part of, one of the first things they do is to search for fellowship. For some that search begins before they leave congregational life; for others it comes after a period of healing, reflection and exploring options.

When leading workshops and conferences for congregations wanting to engage with the findings of this research, I often ask participants to share with one another the aspects of congregational life that they most appreciate. Without fail, they note fellowship and friendship high on their lists and are surprised to learn that what they see as most important is similar to those who have disengaged from church congregations. The difference is not whether these qualities are seen as important. Rather, it is that some people find these in their experience of congregations and others do not. Indeed, what we are learning is that, even in the same congregation, people's experiences differ in significant ways, no doubt coloured by the multiplicity of factors that make us unique and the kinds of dynamics we have touched on that lead to some 'species' being abundant in congregations and others being rare or 'endangered'. The number one stereotype pertaining to church-leavers as 'loners' has no basis in fact. In addition, a growing body of evidence shows that those who characterise themselves as 'spiritual but not religious', although often dismissed as individualists, tend to place a high value on sharing the journey with others.[22]

Taken together, empirical evidence highlights a body that is bigger than many of us had thought. The Christian community is more diverse than is usually considered to be the case. If we were to draw a subset diagram in which one circle signifies the set of 'all regular churchgoers' and another represents the Christian community or 'all followers of Jesus', we now know for sure that the second set is much larger than the first; increasingly, the first group is an important subset of the second.

Regardless of the form our involvement in the Church takes, whether organised or informal, our connectedness is a theological fact and our calling is to express that in lived actuality.

Small connections, big impacts

One of the lessons that environmental rewilding projects have to offer is that small connections can have impacts of disproportionate significance. Take Nigg Bay, for example. Just north of Inverness, there is a sandy bay on the north-east coast of the Cromarty Firth. The north shore is dominated by a huge industrial unit that previously housed an oil platform construction and fabrication yard. As the tide ebbs and flows, vast areas of mudflats, saltmarsh and wet grassland are alternately exposed and submerged, making it a magnet for countless wading birds and wildfowl. With many species finding rich pickings along the tidal fringe, the outgoing flow lures them out towards the sea. As the tide turns the throng is pushed back into the bay. At the peak of mid-winter, the sights and sounds of thousands of pink footed geese, godwits, whooper swans and ducks of

---

22 Aisthorpe, *Invisible Church*, pp. 203–4.

all kinds are astounding, making for one of nature's great spectacles.

The cacophony of whooping swans and honking geese is even more dramatic than it was previously due to a small but significant connection that was made in February 2003. At that time, two 20-metre breaches were made in the sea wall, resulting in a tiny reconnection between a 25-hectare field known as Meddat Marsh and the sea. The wall had cut these habitats off from one another since the 1950s; now they were reconnected. Instead of being sheltered from the sea, the rush-studded field was exposed to the semidiurnal rhythm of the tide. As the twice-daily encroachment of salt water was allowed to resume its impact on the previously 'protected' pasture, intertidal habitats began to develop. Within a year, several key species of saltmarsh plants and mud-dwelling invertebrates had colonised the area. Soon Meddat Marsh had been completely transformed from rush pasture to a mixture of saltmarsh and intertidal mudflats. Those monitoring the impact noted that in the first winter after the reconnection, just three water bird species used the site, but this jumped to nineteen species in the second winter and twenty-five species by 2018.

A seemingly small act of connection can have a profound impact: for that which is directly re-connected and for neighbouring habitats too, as the ripples of change spread.

The Gospel writers tell us that when Jesus sent out his followers he connected them up in pairs or small groups. Some scholars, when reflecting on this, point to stipulations in Old Testament law[23] and Jewish traditions relating to 'two witnesses'. Others point to the common-sense wisdom of Solomon and the profound value of human companionship: 'Two are better than one, because they have a good reward for their toil. For if they fall, one will lift up the other; but woe to one who is alone and falls and does not have another to help. Again, if two lie together, they keep warm; but how can one keep warm alone? And though one might prevail against another, two will withstand one.'[24] In the light of such wisdom, how heartbreaking

23 Deuteronomy 19:15.
24 Ecclesiastes 4:9–12.

to read in the latest in a lengthy catalogue of studies into well-being and resilience among Christian workers, specifically Ministers in the Church of Scotland in this case, the experience of one interviewee: 'I've worked in public, voluntary and private sectors [and] I've never come across such an isolated and unsupervised role in my life.'[25] Of course this reflects the experience of one individual from a large sample, but it also resonates with the findings of similar research in other denominations and Christian organisations spanning several decades. There is a broad seam of research from among people engaged in church-related vocations that consistently points to issues of isolation and difficulty in cultivating and enjoying deep friendships.[26] Of course people involved in formal leadership and ministry roles are a minority in the Church, but this is a symptom of a wider deficit in the Church and the loss of a previous asset.

It was while listening to the experiences of a Christian living on a remote Scottish island that I first heard the term *anam cara*. At that time there were no opportunities to engage with a local congregation, but this person had a vibrant faith and reported, 'What helps me most is an *anam cara* who although in [a place several hundred miles away] is a great help ... I am a long-distance parishioner of [name of a Christian community].' The phrase *anam cara* is an anglicisation of the Irish word *anamchara* and literally means 'soul friend'. From records and accounts from the Celtic tradition it seems that having an *anam cara* was considered normal and essential in Christian living. In the early ninth-century *Martyrology of Oengus the Culdee*,

---

25 Francis, L. J., 2019, *Resilience and Wellbeing in Ministry: An Empirical Enquiry within the Church of Scotland*, https://churchofscotland. org.uk/__data/assets/pdf_file/0008/56825/Resilience_and_Wellbeing_ in_Ministry_-_full_report.pdf, p. 111 (accessed 11.01.2020).

26 For example, Kirk, M. and T. Leary, 1994, *Holy Matrimony? An Exploration of Marriage and Ministry*, Oxford. Lynx highlights 'social isolation' as one of five key factors contributing to stress among clergy; Peyton, N. and C. Gatrell, 2013, in *Managing Clergy Lives: Obedience, Sacrifice, Intimacy*, London: Bloomsbury, argue that many clergy, regardless of marital status, struggle to enjoy friendships, leading to a loss of intimacy and experiences of loneliness.

it is said that one of Ireland's lesser known patron saints, Saint Brigid of Kildare (c. 451–525), told a young man that, just as the water in a well full of lime was good for nothing, so was a person without a soul friend.[27] In a similar vein, Columba's friend Comgall (c. 510/520–597/602), the sixth-century founder of the monastery at Bangor, taught that 'a person without a soul friend is like a body without a head'.[28] Ray Simpson, in his reflections on the life and example of Aidan of Lindisfarne, suggests that the vital role of this relationship of mutual friendship, spiritual mentoring and accountability was lost as the Roman Church gained prominence and confession to priests took its place. Then, following the Protestant Reformation, when reformed churches abandoned confession, the practice of *anam cara* was not reinstated.[29]

Soul friendships have been largely lost to the Church for a very long time, but this habit of cultivating intentional friendship has the potential for a deepening and strengthening out of all proportion to its simplicity. 'Deep friendship is a calling forth of each other's chosenness and a mutual affirmation of being precious in God's eyes,' wrote Henri Nouwen, the twentieth-century Dutch priest and writer on Christian spirituality.[30]

Perhaps this importance of soul friendship is something that the so-called 'invisible church' has to show the more institutional expressions of the Church. In their hunger for fellowship, many are finding rich experiences of friendship and a fertile context for spiritual growth and accountability in informal but intentional meeting with one or two others. I confess that when I first heard Christians who had disengaged from congregational life describe how they were finding fellowship through informal gatherings with one or two friends, I was sceptical about its effectiveness as a strategy for ongoing spiritual growth and enduring fellowship. However, listening to some of those

27 Sellner, E., 1995, 'Soul friendship in early Celtic monasticism', *Aisling Magazine*, 17, Samhain.

28 Simpson, R., 2016, *St Aidan's Way of Mission: Celtic Insights for a post-Christian World*, Abingdon: Bible Reading Fellowship, p. 33.

29 Simpson, *St Aidan's Way of Mission*, p. 36.

30 Nouwen, H., 1992, *Life of the Beloved*, New York, NY: Crossroad, p. 65.

people five years on from first making contact, I am both encouraged and challenged by the depth of relationships that has developed and the opportunities that these friendships afford to share with others who have yet to discover Christian life. One such person, disengaged from congregational life for nearly twenty years, described his main fellowship as 'meeting with Christian friends ... sometimes of course we'll involve some element of liturgy and exploration ... a lot of discussion' and looks back on involvement in a more formal setting as '... it was really comfortable, it was great and friendly and warm and very supportive but it lacked relevance to what we did the rest of the week. It was quite inward looking, so although we talked a lot about discipleship [and] there was a lot of preaching about that, the actual opportunities to live that out were more limited within that model.'

Rowan Williams, once head of one of the largest church institutions in the world, has come to see that, however Church is expressed, at a basic level it comprises people who recognise one another as 'gifts'. So, for example, he suggests that whenever we meet another Christian we should view them as a gift from Christ and be eager and curious as to what we might learn from them or through them. '... Believing in the Church is really believing in the unique gift of the other that God has given you to live with.'[31] Likewise, we ourselves are a unique gift to the Church and to those God brings across our path: ' ... my act must be a gift for the deepening and strengthening of another's faith'.[32] The kind of friendships that emerge from this viewing of one another as gifts are a blessing to one another, but also shape the Church 'as a community in which each person has a gift that only they can give into the common life'.[33]

---

31 Williams, R., 2007, *Tokens of Trust: An Introduction to Christian Belief*, Louisville, KY: Westminster John Knox Press, p. 106.

32 Williams, R., 2000, *On Christian Theology*, Oxford: Blackwell, p. 285.

33 Williams, *On Christian Theology*, p. 285.

For those who long for a rewilding of the Church, can there be a more efficacious starting point than the rediscovery of soul friendships?

Daylighting our rivers

Across the UK and around the world, rivers have been forced to flow underground as cities have developed. During the industrial revolution, for reasons of sanitation, partly just to conceal the stench and often to enable the squeezing of more buildings into already crowded towns and cities, rivers were covered over. With the biggest rivers this was not possible, but smaller rivers disappeared from urban landscapes. You would never guess, but Sheffield, for example, is built around a network of rivers. As they degenerated into sewers in the late nineteenth century, they were forced into systems of hidden channels. But change is coming. Until recently, except for a brief glimpse of it disappearing into a culvert, Porter Brook was concealed from view, disconnected from the surrounding landscape and invisible to the local population. Now, what was previously a crumbling car park is a 'green amphitheatre, sloping down to the banks of the river, where wild trout spawn in spring'.[34]

'Daylighting' is the process of re-opening rivers to the sky, peeling back their manmade coverings and reuniting rivers with life above and around. On the international stage a much-feted daylighting project is Seoul's Cheonggyecheon river. A brainwave of then-mayor and future president Lee Myung-bak, the project drew back the tarmac and concrete shrouds of long-buried streams to create an almost four-mile-long channel of water. In addition to the aesthetic and environmental benefits, it is credited with substantial flood-relief benefits and even 'transforming an area of Seoul previously renowned for crime'.[35] The

---

34 Cox, D., 2017, 'A river runs through it: the global movement to "daylight" urban waterways', *The Guardian*, 29 August, www.theguardian.com/cities/2017/aug/29/river-runs-global-movement-day-light-urban-rivers (accessed 06.01.2020).

35 Cox, 'A river runs through it'.

UK is a little late to the daylighting party. Switzerland, North America and New Zealand have been reconnecting with the life-giving streams below their cities for some time. But we are making a start, with some of the towns and cities most transformed by heavy industry in the past benefiting from the re-creation of much-needed water-fringed green spaces. As concrete is peeled away, rivers are being allowed to reconnect to the surrounding ecosystems and we are able to reconnect with them.

In *Streams of Living Water*, Richard Foster argues that, undergirding the emergence and decline of the sweeping historical movements within the Church, six 'Great Traditions' can be identified.[36] At different phases in our history, a renewed emphasis on one or other of these traditions has reshaped the Church. Aspects of the Church's identity and calling that have been blind spots come into fresh focus. The Contemplative Tradition highlights the centrality of prayer, the Holiness Tradition emphasises the importance of the formation of Christian character, and the Charismatic Tradition focuses attention on the Spirit-empowered life. As different ones have gained prominence, new manifestations of the Church have arisen, existing expressions have been reformed and schisms have led to new branches developing. The Social Justice Tradition reminds Christians of their vocation to be a transforming influence in every sphere of life, the Evangelical Tradition emphasises the foundational role of the Scriptures, and the Incarnational Tradition gives particular attention to how we encounter the invisible God in the visible world or, in other words, the 'sacramental life'.

If the Church were viewed as a giant tree, these 'Great Traditions' would be the underlying streams that have been the sources of new life and revived vision. The history of denominations and networks can be traced in terms of renewed awakenings to one or other emphasis and becoming less aware of others. At different times the great tree's roots dive down into one stream while withdrawing from others.

---

36 Foster, R., 1998, *Streams of Living Water*, London: HarperCollins.

If, instead of picturing the whole Church as a single tree, we think of different denominations and groups as being different kinds of tree, we can see that these species have different patterns of root growth. Some have a noticeable 'tap root', a primary root, and other secondary or tertiary roots, each drawing nourishment from one of the streams of tradition. Others, particularly older species, have broad root systems anchored in all of the traditions, though perhaps without a passionate grip on any one in particular. To take the analogy a little further, just as the root system of a tree is strongly influenced by the qualities of the soil in which it grows, we can see how the Church's development is shaped by local contexts. Factors in the prevailing culture shape the Church's development, luring it in certain ways and challenging its growth in other directions.

The direction of prevailing winds is reflected in the root systems of trees. As strong winds batter a tree from a predominant direction, the roots that secure it on that windward side are strained and stretched, loosening the surrounding soil, allowing and stimulating the roots on that side to dive deeper and grow stronger. Easy conditions for growth, loose soil and moderate winds may produce beautiful symmetry in a root system, but are unlikely to create resilient and sturdy trees. It tends to be powerful winds from unusual directions that are responsible for blowing down trees, and when that happens the root system on the usually leeward side offers a vision of stunted frailty.

We are privileged to live in the twenty-first century. The two-millennia perspective of the Church that is available to us means that there is no excuse for blinkered development of one or two of the great traditions of the Church and neglect of others. A quotation attributed to the author and film director Michael Crichton is salutary for Christians and especially those involved in the leadership and development of any kind of Christian community: 'If you don't know history, then you don't know anything. You are a leaf that doesn't know it is part of a tree.' We live at a time when denominational edifices are crumbling. Recent generations have little interest in theological siloes or ecclesiastical brand loyalty. It is time for our own radical daylighting projects, peeling away religious labels and stereotypes, opening up and reconnecting with all of the streams that carry the riches of our faith from one generation to the next. Exploring traditions that are unfamiliar to us is not an academic exercise, although we may well want to start by extending our reading beyond the sources that reinforce our current perspectives. There is benefit in consciously choosing to explore viewpoints that will challenge. If we are part of a congregation, we might want to invite people from other traditions to teach and share their experiences. For all of us, retreat centres, festivals, online communities and parachurch organisations offer opportunities to experience practices from traditions to which we are unaccustomed, to 'daylight' streams that may have been concealed from us, to help us to open ourselves to be refreshed and renewed by them.

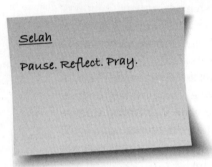

Selah

Pause. Reflect. Pray.

Intouchness and intactness

It took me completely by surprise. My wife and I were on holiday in the Netherlands. It had been an enthralling week. Under the tutelage of our Dutch friends we had begun to understand how the aspirations of their ancestors and the power of the wind had wrested hundreds of thousands of hectares of rich agricultural land from the clutches of the North Sea and its swampy eastern fringe. We had been enchanted by the polychromatic oceans of tulips and delighted by their cycle-rich, vehicle-sparse cities. But this I was not expecting.

We were hurtling along the *snelweg*, a Dutch motorway, and suddenly there it was. Floating over the bustle and blare, the noise and noxious vapours of a major traffic artery was ... a slice of Eden. As on any major European road we had already passed under a multitude of overpasses; bridges carrying roads and railways had criss-crossed our route at regular intervals. But this was different. Here was an arc of forest, sweeping *over* the multi-lane highway. In stark contrast to the regimented ranks of poplars that stand to attention along the dykes and canals in the landscapes of the Dutch and Flemish Masters and remain characteristic of the Low Countries today, here was a dense swathe of mature trees above our heads. Even to my amateur's eye it appeared to comprise an assortment of coniferous and deciduous trees, carpeted with an understory of grasses and bushy shrubs. And it wasn't just a narrow strip, but a similar width to the multi-lane highway below. Our host explained that this was an 'ecoduct', sometimes known as green bridges or wildlife crossings.

I had heard of underpasses in the UK designed to enable hedgehogs to avoid going the way of their 'flat mates' (sorry!) on the roads above. Close to my home there is an area where thick ropes have been slung above a road to enable red squirrels to avoid the same fate. Actually, while they go largely unnoticed, Britain's road network is riddled with tunnels and culverts specifically for the protection of amphibians, otters, hedgehogs, badgers and other species. When I was a child it seemed ironic that Tufty Fluffytail, a cartoon squirrel, should teach the children of Britain the Green Cross Code. Road-kill-littered roads were clear evidence of the ineptitude of small mammals when it comes to pedestrian road safety. Now it seems that they have progressed to their own network of pelican crossing equivalents.

Anyway, the ecoduct I saw in the Netherlands and dozens like it are more than just safe alternatives to crossing dangerous roads. They are part of a growing network of infrastructure designed to counter the negative impacts of other infrastructure. If you are imagining narrow overpasses or slender culverts, think again. The one I saw was no exception, it seems; indeed it was one of the more modest examples. Its big brother, the Natuurbrug Zanderij Crailoo, built in 2006, is 50 metres wide, nearly a kilometre long and traverses a business park and a sports complex as well as a river, a road and a railway line.

In a country with a population density approaching five hundred people per square kilometre, ecologists have realised that the habitats of all kinds of wildlife, from plants and insects to larger mammals, are carved into 'islands' of ever-diminishing size. The study of what has become known as 'island biogeography'[37] has shown how the isolation of natural communities, whether it be fish, plants, insects or mammals, affects the health and population of a species. To a beetle, a partridge or a pine marten, their home does not need to be surrounded by water to become an 'island'. An 'island' is created whenever any area of habitat suitable for a specific species becomes surrounded by unsuitable habitat, creating a situation where a limited genetic pool leads to an inevitable spiral of decline.

The 2016 *State of Nature* report, perhaps the most thorough account of the UK's natural heritage, pools data and expertise from more than fifty nature conservation and research organisations to give an overview of the health of ecosystems in the UK. It explains the shocking fact that out of 218 nations, the UK ranks 189th for the 'intactness' of its living systems. Ecological scientists have developed a Biodiversity Intactness Index (BII) which estimates the average abundance of originally present species relative to their abundance in undisturbed habitat. The most 'developed' countries are realising that they have some of the most fragmented and fractured environments. As we reconnect with nature and realise that we are part of it, we are also waking up to the urgent need for, and disproportionate benefits of, reconnecting habitats.

Another recent report on intactness was published by Demos,[38] the cross-party think tank that specialises in developing evidence-based social policy in the areas of health, education and housing. This report, however, was about the interconnectedness of society and, in particular, the involvement of Christian faith-based communities in wider society. It reports

---

37 MacArthur, R. and E. Wilson, 1967, *The Theory of Island Biogeography*, Princeton, NJ: Princeton University Press. Island biogeography is now often termed 'insular biogeography'.

38 Barclay, D. and S. Hilhorst, 2019, *Holy Alliances: Church-Secular Partnerships for Social Good*, Demos, pp. 4–5.

good news. One aspect of God's rewilding of the Church is a reconnecting of those who follow the Jesus way with their own communities and wider society. Demos's *Holy Alliances* report reveals that in the decade since the financial crisis of 2007–8, there has been notable growth in church-based social action. Their previous *Faithful Citizens* report[39] got considerable newspaper coverage in 2013, when it demonstrated that religious people in the UK were significantly more likely to volunteer regularly in their local community. At that time some observers, not unreasonably, suggested that a lot of that volunteering was likely to be within their own religious community and for the benefit of that community. However, this more recent report demonstrates that the picture is altogether more generous and more orientated towards the wider community than cynics previously suggested.

The Demos findings demonstrate that, 'driven both by the "pull" of austerity and the "push" of social theology'[40] many churches are creating connections with other organisations in order to better serve their communities. They found that nearly a quarter (23 per cent) of churches are forging partnerships with non-faith voluntary organisations. Significant numbers of churches are collaborating with local authorities (17 per cent) and schools (17 per cent). Others are joining hands with businesses, health organisations and the police in tackling food poverty, mental health and other social challenges. The overall picture is that not only are churches connecting with others, but at a time when many churches are struggling to maintain their own legal compliance, governance structures, programme of worship services etc., they are also doing more of it. A survey conducted by Jubilee Plus[41] showed that church volunteer

---

39 Birdwell, J. (ed.), 2013, *The Faith Collection*, London: Demos. Retrieved from www.demos.co.uk/files/DEMOS_The_Faith_Collection_-_web_version.pdf?1379811908 (accessed 08.01.2020).

40 Barclay, D. and S. Hilhorst, *Holy Alliances: Church-Secular Partnerships for Social Good*, London: Demos, p. 4. Retrieved from https://demos.co.uk/wp-content/uploads/2019/09/Holy-Alliances-digital-final-.pdf (accessed 7.01.20).

41 Knott, G., 2014, *Investing More in the Common Good*, Shrewsbury: Jubilee Plus. Retrieved from https://jubilee-plus.org/docs/Report-

hours spent on social action had reached a whopping 114.8 million hours per year by 2014 and that this represented an increase of almost 60 per cent since 2010. The Cinnamon Network's *Faith Action Audit*[42] in 2016 valued the Church's volunteering effort in the UK at over £3 billion per year. This pattern of increasing net volume of volunteering by churches is reflected in a host of similar data sources. The Church Urban Fund found that over 90 per cent of churches in England in 2014 were addressing at least one social issue in their local area;[43] two years later the Theos report *Doing Good: A Future for Christianity in the 21st Century*[44] estimated that 10 million adults in the UK used church-based community services.

As with much research into Christian activities these reports tend to limit their scope to people who are members of formal congregations, but studies among other Christians show a similar picture of widespread social involvement. In one study, 40 per cent reported regular involvement with 'non-church clubs, organisations or groups'.

Street Pastors and Street Angels are a good example of the kind of rapid development and collaborative modality that Demos and others have highlighted. The genesis of Street Pastors was a handful of church volunteers in Brixton, London in 2003. 'Street Pastors is about Christians rolling up their sleeves and getting involved in practically responding to the problems of crime and safety,' says David Burrowes, Patron of Ascension Trust. Two years later a similar group in Halifax, West Yorkshire, became the seed for the Street Angels network, a similar organisation. Both draw Christians from many traditions and work closely with the police, town centre

---

National-Church-Social-Action-Survey-2014-Executive-Summary.pdf (accessed 05.01.2020).

42 Cinnamon Network, 2016, *Faith Action Audit*. Retrieved from www.cinnamonnetwork.co.uk/wp-content/uploads/2016/08/Cinnamon-Faith-Action-Audit-Report-2016.pdf (accessed 05.01.2020).

43 Church Urban Fund, 2015, *Church in Action*. Retrieved from www.cuf.org.uk/church-in-action-2015 (accessed 05.01.2020).

44 Spencer, N., 2016, *Doing Good: A Future for Christianity in the 21st Century*, London: Theos. Retrieved from www.theosthinktank.co.uk/files/files/Doing%20Good%205.pdf (accessed 05.01.2020).

management and a range of other organisations. At the time of writing, over 300 towns and cities around the UK have a Street Pastors team. There is a strong commitment to prayer and the emergence of these groups has been linked to falls in crime and positive changes in the culture of night-time town and city centres.

Drawing new inspiration and strength from streams of living water, investing in relationships of mutual support and accountability, re-connecting with wider society: this is life in the kingdom; this is rewilding the Church. And, while connecting to sources of life, we also need to name and confront those things that smother, divert or drain away life and diversity. It's time to uproot the invasive species.

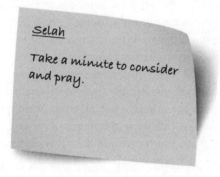

Selah

Take a minute to consider and pray.

9

RELEASE: Culling the Invasive Species

So then, let us rid ourselves of everything
that gets in the way ...
Hebrews 12:1 (GNT)

The devastating impact of invasive species

From the sixteenth century onwards, hunters decimated the Galápagos giant tortoise. Ironically, one of the most extraordinary adaptations of these remarkable creatures was part of the reason for their near demise. Their ability to survive without food and water for up to a year made them ideal sources of fresh meat on long voyages. Even the great naturalist Charles Darwin took more than thirty tortoises on his ship, *The Beagle*, as food for the voyage to Polynesia. However, while the impact of hunting was devastating, it was the invasive species that the hunters introduced inadvertently that almost forced the tortoise into extinction. Rice rats in particular led to the annihilation of some tortoise species and pushed others to the brink. At one point, the remaining fourteen of one particular species, the Española, were collected by conservationists, before non-native rats and other pests could exterminate this fragile remnant. Then, over several years, an intensive programme of invasive species eradication rehabilitated the habitat of the Galápagos tortoise. The Española was reintroduced in 2010 and, without the invidious influence of invasive species, they have flourished. At the time of writing, a healthy population of over 1,500 individuals has been re-established and is growing.

In the world of ecology, terminology around invasive species is hotly contested. Academic papers make careful distinctions between species that are 'alien', 'colonising', 'escaped', 'endemic established', 'exotic foreign immigrants', 'naturalised', 'noxious', 'nuisance', 'transient', 'waif' ... and the list goes on. To the lay person it may seem bizarre that scholars spill so much ink about what amount of damage is needed to be inflicted on the native ecosystem for a plant or animal to be branded 'invasive'. And yet perhaps it is not so surprising. After all, ask any two gardeners which plants are 'weeds' and which are 'flowers' and you are likely to receive answers that are different, but impassioned all the same. All would agree that the former should be eliminated and the latter nurtured, but which species belong on which side of the dividing lines would be the subject of fervent debate.

In the same way, it would be naïve to suggest that identifying which values, practices and cultural characteristics constitute invasive pests in the Christian community is straightforward. Yes, just as gardeners in the UK would be unanimous in branding Japanese knotweed an unwelcome alien, Christians of all persuasions would find no difficulty in agreeing on some extreme examples and there would be little point in identifying them here. However, there are others that, whether on the basis of theological reflection or empirical evidence, are hostile to spiritual thriving and contrary to the health of Christian community – and yet are sufficiently well disguised in the context of contemporary culture that, just like some exotic plants become 'naturalised', they become established as acceptable or even desirable.

In keeping with our rewilding metaphor, in this chapter we will explore some of the more noxious and yet also cunningly camouflaged nuisances that derail our journey into greater Christlikeness and undermine the health and growth of the Church. For example, Jesus was uncompromising and insistent that unless King Mammon is dethroned, Christian integrity is impossible.[1] Likewise, these other invasive aliens

---

1 Matthew 6:24.

also need to be uprooted and exterminated if the kingdom is to thrive.[2]

My overwhelming sense is that, for the kingdom that Jesus proclaimed and demonstrated to flourish and expand, we don't need to *do* more and we don't need to be cleverer; it is neither ingenious tactics nor a nifty strategy that is required. Rather, having heard his call afresh, we need to respond by culling what is unhelpful, live lives of simple and courageous obedience, and trust God that what emerges will reflect the splendour of his kingdom. Our task is not to grow God's Church for him. When Paul explained, 'I planted, Apollos watered, but God gave the growth',[3] he was neither denying nor demeaning the role of those who are called and gifted to pioneer and nurture Christian communities. Rather, he is calling for appropriate humility, as the renovation of hearts and building of Church are beyond human endeavour.

As I have explained elsewhere,[4] it seems that a fundamental misunderstanding of what Church is and isn't lies at the root of much misapplied energy and needless anguish. The purpose of Church is not to preserve or propagate the Church. Neither is it the preservation of religious traditions. As followers of Jesus, it's all about him and his kingdom. That is what we live for. The writer to the Hebrews makes a simple two-fold plea to the hearers and readers of his message: first, 'throw off everything that hinders and the sin that so easily entangles'; second, 'fixing our eyes on Jesus ... run the race'.[5]

Advocates of rewilding trust that culling or eradicating invasive species and then allowing the inherent processes of nature to have their way will result in a vibrant, sustainable and authentic landscape. It involves actively exterminating what impedes biodiversity and being intentionally passive about

2 Although Jesus never gave a neat definition of the kingdom, his meaning is clear in the first request of what we often call the Lord's Prayer: 'Thy kingdom come, Thy will be done in earth, as it is in heaven' (Matthew 6:10).

3 1 Corinthians 3:6.

4 Aisthorpe, S., 2016, *The Invisible Church*, Edinburgh: Saint Andrew Press, pp. 111–12.

5 Hebrews 12:1–2 (NIV).

what then emerges. Rewilding the Church requires no less and no more than a rejecting of 'everything that hinders' and a renewed commitment to a courageous following of Christ. It requires Christian leaders to deliberately take their hands off the steering wheel and to choose to sit on their hands in order to give space for 'natural processes' to go ahead unhindered. This chapter will attempt to unpack what may sound to some naïve and simplistic. However, perhaps on reflection what appears simplistic will be just simple. Perhaps with further consideration, what seems naïve is ... well, just that – naïve, another term for childlike trust.

Biotic potential

It seems that the apostle Paul had a sense of what biologists now term 'biotic potential'. This is the inborn, instinctive potential of a living thing to grow and reproduce under optimum conditions. Small, simple organisms tend to have the highest biotic potential. In ideal conditions, a single *E. coli* bacterium can reproduce nearly one million cells. In contrast, a blue whale, even in an optimal environment, grows and produces offspring at such a slow rate that its biotic potential is tiny. Of course, reaching full biotic potential is rarely if ever possible. Perhaps the only times we come close to seeing it is in a petri dish in laboratory conditions. Usually biotic potential is suppressed by 'environmental resistance', the multitude of factors that inhibit growth and reproduction, including, of course, the impacts of populations of other organisms in the same ecosystem.

Paul had witnessed the extraordinary biotic potential of the Church unleashed as communities of faith sprang up and multiplied even in the most aggressive and hostile environments. He urged people to recognise the 'immeasurable greatness of [God's] power' at work within and among them, identifying that potential as being from the same source and in the same measure as the mighty power involved in the resurrection of Jesus.[6] It is tempting to wonder what kind of environmental

---

6 Ephesians 1:19–20.

resistance could possibly tame such colossal power and yet here is the paradox. The invasive species that hamper and undermine rewilding the Church are not violent persecution or rampant heresy. Indeed they may sound innocuous, humdrum even, and that is part of their terrifying threat.

In our playful and yet serious use of the metaphor of rewilding, the culling of intrusive species is a helpful representation for 'throwing off everything that hinders'. But, let's be clear – in using the metaphor in this way, we are never talking about 'throwing off' individual people. These invasive weeds or poisonous pests are the harmful habits we might adopt and, in particular, the toxic characteristics of church cultures we may inhabit and collude with. They are enemies of rewilding because they undermine our awareness of our (and others') identity as beloved, inhibit our wholehearted response to the invitation of Jesus and constrain our 'walk'[7] in ways that can reduce it to a frustrated stumble. They may sound innocent, but do not be fooled: they carry a spiritual health warning. The threat level is critical. The discussion of some of the harmful habits and toxic cultures that follows is a red warning: damage is being caused, power cuts are guaranteed, loss of life is likely.

The noxious impact of the frenetic

When I run workshops for church congregations, there is invariably both pleasant surprise and a tangible sense of relief as I explain that the outcome of our deliberations will not be 'more work'. Likewise, when I state that, in my experience, most congregations operate on the outer edge of what is possible with the resources at their disposal, especially when it comes to the time and energy that people are able to devote to organisational activities, there are noises and body language that communicate the recognition of the truth of this within

---

7 Throughout the New Testament, especially in Paul's epistles, the verb 'walk' is used metaphorically to refer to a lifestyle that emerges from faith in Jesus: a 'new life' (Romans 6:4), marked by love (Ephesians 5:2), wisdom (Colossians 4:5) and truth (3 John 4).

the listeners' own experience. Frenetic activity is an invasive species within the Church. It is not only the enemy of personal thriving, it also leads to organisational cultures in which joy is suffocated and innovation is inhibited.

In my work listening to those who have disengaged from congregational life I often hear that, following an initial experience of grief, there is a sense of relief at having stepped off what felt like an organisational treadmill. While it is usual that, for a while at least, church-leavers lament losses of various kinds, typically they then report a sense of liberation from what had become a burden of tasks and duties that seemed to undermine their spiritual well-being and divert energy from what they perceive to be their vocation or optimum application of their gifts. One person expressed their experience of practising their faith beyond the context of a congregation in these terms:

> I think the overwhelming experience is of a much better ... 'equilibrium' ... there's a sense of being in the right place, doing the right things, which really helps, I think, take the opportunities of the time and the talents and the gifts that we've been given.

One participant in the *Faith Journeys Beyond the Congregations* study,[8] struggling to articulate what he had experienced during his years of involvement as an elder and youth leader, quoted Bilbo Baggins in J. R. R. Tolkien's *The Fellowship of the Ring*: 'I felt thin, sort of stretched, like butter scraped over too much bread.' And, of course, in that analogy there are two ways of overcoming that sense of being stretched thin. One is to have more butter; the other is to reduce the area of bread. However, when butter is analogous to people and their capacities, there are no shortcuts to an increased supply and, in the struggle to stretch restricted resources ever-thinner, patterns of thinking can take root which exacerbate rather than alleviate the situation. Those who feel that they carry a

---

8 Aisthorpe, S., 2013, *Faith Journeys Beyond the Congregations*, Church of Scotland Mission and Discipleship Council. Retrieved from www.resourcingmission.org.uk/resources/faith-journeys-beyondcongre gations.

particularly heavy burden can become resentful of others who appear less committed or active in congregational life. Others may feel aggrieved at the idea that they need to increase their involvement if they are not to be seen as nominal or not pulling their weight. Those who believe that their calling requires their time to be focused beyond the congregation or group can feel misunderstood or undermined by expectations or demands to focus their energies on congregational life over their perceived priorities. Usually subconscious and rarely stated explicitly, such thought patterns nonetheless can feed off one another and create a culture that becomes introspective and judgemental. Another interviewee in one of the studies among Christians who are not engaged with a local church congregation, typical of those who identified this as one of the key factors in their decision to move away from congregational life, described their experience as follows:

> I think one thing that I found hardest of all in the church was the criticism of other Christians ... There seemed to be a growing preoccupation of people with criticising others and I found that it was making me critical too. It just seemed to be the spiral of judging and criticising people was snowballing – it was just getting worse and I didn't want to be in that position. I didn't want to be someone that was judgemental and critical of people.[9]

This kind of observation from among the many who have disengaged from churches has an interesting relationship with the evidence of those who have analysed data from congregations that are thriving. In a previous chapter, I mentioned Robert Warren's discovery that Anglican churches that were bucking the trend and experiencing numerical growth and thriving displayed a small number of notable characteristics.[10] As well as the characteristic 'Seek to find out what God wants ... discern the Spirit's leading rather than trying to please everyone'

---

9 Aisthorpe, *Faith Journeys Beyond the Congregations.*
10 Warren, R., 2012, *The Healthy Church Handbook*, London: Church House Publishing.

already mentioned, another mark of a healthy church identified through their research was 'Does a few things and does them well'. In practice, this mark of congregational life is the outcome of the aforementioned seeking, listening and discerning. When the life and activity of a congregation or group grow naturally from corporate listening and discernment, the pressure to please everyone is replaced with a commitment to a shared vision, the frenetic by a common focus.

Certainly my own experience confirms that, whatever positive qualities a congregation or group may have, these are undermined if there is a culture of frenetic activity. In helping congregations to discern their future, it is always my hope that they will be excited about what they are going to be and do, but, equally, that they will be relaxed and guilt-free about what they are *not* going to do. Being explicit about 'planned neglect' is essential if we are to escape the relentless plea to do more. The Companions of Brother Lawrence, an ecumenical fellowship inspired by the example of Brother Lawrence of the Resurrection (c. 1614–1691),[11] have the following wisdom at the heart of their Rule of Life: 'For us, planned neglect will mean deliberately choosing which things we will leave undone or postpone, so that instead of being oppressed by a clutter of unfinished jobs, we think out our priorities under God and then accept without guilt or resentment the fact that much we had thought we ought to do we must leave.'

I said above that in the analogy of the butter and the bread there are two ways of overcoming that sense of being stretched thin. This, then, is the second way and, in a scenario where butter is a finite resource, the only real option – planned neglect on the basis of prayerful discernment – is deciding carefully which bread to cover. There is genuine joy in being confident in one's calling and recognising that competing demands, however apparently worthwhile, are distractions to be politely and firmly declined. We live at a time when social media fuels the rampant social anxiety mentioned previously, the so-called

---

11 Brother Lawrence's exhortation to simple and Christ-centred living, *The Practice of the Presence of God*, has become a classic of Christian spirituality.

'Fear of Missing Out' (FOMO).[12] Concern that others might be having experiences from which they are absent means that some people experience a genuine discomfort if they fail to stay continually connected and, as far as possible, involved with what others are doing. It's a twenty-first-century incarnation of 'keeping up with the Joneses'. It feeds a culture of frenetic activity and, far from being immune, church congregations and institutions are easily drawn into the same kind of whirl-pool of activity, where it is hard to believe that doing less could possibly deliver benefits. The counter-cultural response has been articulated well by Australian cultural commentator and cartoonist Michael Leunig, whose poem 'JOMO (Joy of Missing Out)' celebrates a lifestyle of simplicity and a Christ-like attitude to acquisitiveness, whether material or otherwise:

Oh the joy of missing out.
When the world begins to shout
And rush towards that shining thing;
The latest bit of mental bling –
Trying to have it, see it, do it,
You simply know you won't go through it;
The anxious clamouring and need
This restless hungry thing to feed ...[13]

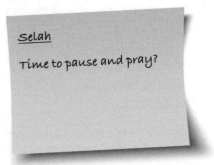

Selah

Time to pause and pray?

12 Przybylski, Andrew K. and colleagues, 2013, 'Motivational, emo-tional, and behavioral correlates of fear of missing out', *Computers in Human Behavior*, July 29(4), pp. 1841–8.

13 Leunig, M., 2017, 'JOMO', *Leunig*, 15 July, www.leunig.com.au/works/recent-cartoons/769-jomo.

The poisonous pest of busyness

Frenetic activity lacks focus; 'busyness' refers to the sheer volume of action, living close to the edge of one's capacity with minimal 'margin'. In a particularly poignant scene in the 1994 film *The Shawshank Redemption*, Brooks Hatlan, an elderly man recently released after decades of incarceration, writes to his friends back in jail about his sense of bewilderment and isolation in the face of the world as it has become: 'Dear fellas, I can't believe how fast things move on the outside ... The world went and got itself in a big damn hurry.' In his revealing study of modern living, *The Great Acceleration: How the World is Getting Faster, Faster*, Robert Colvile explores the evolutionary science behind the many and varied ways in which the pace of life is increasing.[14] Apparently, a fundamental fact of human behaviour is that people in larger communities move faster. A child raised in a city races around a supermarket considerably faster than their country cousin. Colvile observes a positive link between faster lives and productivity, but also asks whether our bodies, minds and the natural environment can cope.

Most years, national newspapers in the UK feature reports and editorials based on research regarding changing patterns of working hours. The trend is invariably in one direction. One of this year's headlines, typical of many, reads 'British workers put in longest hours in EU, study finds ... German and Danish workers more productive than UK counterparts even though they work fewer hours, says TUC'.[15] Although we generally work fewer hours and have longer holidays than our sisters and brothers in the USA, we work longer days and take less annual leave than most of Europe. The average German has already been home for an hour before we leave work. Including bank holidays, UK workers get an average of 28 days holiday

---

14 Colvile, R., 2016, *The Great Acceleration: How the World is Getting Faster, Faster*, London: Bloomsbury.

15 Jones, A., 2019, 'British workers put in longest hours in EU, study finds', 17 April, *Independent*, www.independent.co.uk/news/business/news/british-workers-hours-put-in-longest-hours-in-eu-study-finds-a8872971.html (accessed 11.09.2019).

each year, compared to the 47 days per year enjoyed by our neighbours in France.

In addition to the extra time spent at our places of employment, the nature of work is becoming intensified and less relational. Our average commute times are the longest in Europe. In the most recent studies, half of us admit to feeling busier now than twelve months ago and 41 per cent say they have less free time than a decade ago. More than four in ten of us (43 per cent) feel we can never switch off from work because of the amount of emails we monitor on smartphones.

And what about church? Is it a therapeutic break from the busyness of the rest of life or do we import our addiction to busyness into church life? Is part of the underlying cause of the frenetic activity discussed above a subconscious need to be busy? And if so, why might that be? Although Robert Colvile does not address explicitly the challenges facing church institutions, his observations will resonate for many: 'All of us are busy being useful. The more there is to worry about professional and institutional survival, the more useful we seek to be … Such an effort at usefulness may rob us of vitality.'[16] One root of our busyness seems to be a kind of institutional angst, a deep concern that things might go awry on our watch.

Increasingly, when facilitating workshops to help congregations to discern their future direction, I choose to minimise the language of what do we need to 'do' and place more emphasis on 'who does God want us to *be*?' If our diagnosis is that church institutions are declining because of church failings, and that the future demands that we save them, then a reasonable prescription is greater effort, more resolve, more busyness. But what if God is *in* some of the changes that concern us? What if the movement from institutional to organic, from complex to simple, from large to small, is not a downward slide to be resisted, but a way to follow, a pathway along which we encounter the footprints of Christ? If this is the diagnosis then busyness needs to be replaced with what Eugene Peterson calls 'willed passivity'. It's a term that sounds self-contradictory, but describes well the reality of rewilding, a deliberate and inten-

---

16 Colvile, *The Great Acceleration*, p. 238.

tional passivity that creates the space for natural processes to prosper. Peterson contrasts the 'indolent, inattentive passivity that approximates the existence of a slug' with 'a willed and attentive passivity that is something like worship'.[17]

Tim Chester, the author of *The Busy Christian's Guide to Busyness*, points out that another reason Christians end up so busy is that we are tempted, in his words, to have 'a foot in both camps'. That is, on the one hand, we want our lives to be 'poured out'[18] as an offering to Christ and throw ourselves into personal devotion and Christian activity. But then, being in the words of James, 'double-minded people',[19] we also want all the world has to offer. 'We work hard for the treasure of heaven. But we also work hard for the treasure of earth. So we're running around twice as much as the pagans.'[20]

A friend quipped recently, 'We run around, busily creating a draught, and trying to convince ourselves that it is the wind of the Spirit!' It may have been a light-hearted comment, but it was actually an astute and terrifying observation. Eugene Peterson, always insightful and never one to pull his punches, suggests that there is a pandemic of busyness among Christian leaders. With the shocking and laser-sharp accuracy reserved for someone who cultivates sufficient unbusyness to be able to wait in prayer and speak and write from a place of confidence, he states that 'busy', when used to describe a 'pastor', 'should sound to our ears like ... embezzling to describe a banker'.[21] It is, he continues, 'an outrageous scandal, a blasphemous affront'. Although Peterson is writing about 'pastors' and in the context of North America, I would extend his observation to include all who hope to properly discern God's activity and their faithful part within that. Perhaps using the term *blasphemous* to describe a busy Christian leader may be so dramatic that it runs the risk of not being taken seriously. However, consider

---

17 Peterson, E., 1993, *The Contemplative Pastor*, Grand Rapids, MI: Eerdmans, p. 107.

18 Philippians 2:17.

19 James 1:8.

20 Chester, T., 2006, *The Busy Christian's Guide to Busyness*, London: IVP, p. 129.

21 Peterson, *The Contemplative Pastor*, p. 17.

for a moment what that word actually means. Surely blasphemy describes behaviour that either denies God what is right and proper – or attributes to God that which is erroneous and unfitting. With that meaning in mind, perhaps his shocking statement warrants closer consideration. If accusing the busy pastor of blasphemy were not sufficiently shocking, Peterson underscores his point by suggesting that 'the word busy is the synonym not of commitment but of betrayal. It is not devotion but defection.'[22]

Digging out the roots of the invaders

Himalayan balsam is beautiful. Brought to our shores in 1839 to adorn the gardens of the aristocracy, the Victorian craze for 'wild gardening' soon saw its seeds passed around by enthusiasts. By the 1850s this hardy and eye-catching species had escaped the confines of managed gardens and entered the wider ecosystem. One of the novel characteristics of the Himalayan balsam is its 'ballistic dispersal' of seeds. Its explosive seed capsule scatters seeds over several metres. Like amphibious landing craft, seeds float down water courses, pushing the combat zone of balsam's domination ever onwards, establishing dense beds that shade out and crowd out many native species. Attracted by its copious nectar, pollinating insects are drawn to beds of balsam to the detriment of other flowering plants. To release the strangling grip of this invasive pest, to enable rewilding of the riverbanks and damp woodlands they have come to control, to allow biodiversity to flourish, it has to be uprooted. People on the frontline of the battle against balsam know that the only hope of relinquishing its stubborn grasp is to dig down and drag it from the ground.

In his unmasking of busyness as an invasive species, Peterson suggests two deep and tenacious roots. 'I become busy for two reasons,' he confesses, 'both ignoble.' The first he suggests is vanity. Self-worth is a deep human craving. We want to appear important to others. We want to feel that we are significant. Of

---

22 Peterson, *The Contemplative Pastor*, p. 17.

course, the truth is that we are important; we are significant; before we do anything we are the apple of the Almighty's eye. It was *before* the ministry of Jesus got started that he heard the voice from heaven: 'You are my Son, the Beloved; with you I am well pleased.'[23] Likewise, we are chosen and loved, not because of anything we do and often despite it. Sadly, however, we often embrace the lie that even to be appreciated, let alone be loved, we need to achieve. The observation that we are human *beings* and not human *doings* has become a cliché, but actually contains a profound truth. When, in his old age, the apostle John reflected on a lifetime of Christian living he reminded his brothers and sisters that, 'We love because he first loved us.'[24] When our activity is motivated by a deep gratitude for all we receive as the beloved of God, we draw from the bottomless well of grace. When our underlying motive is a need to earn the esteem of others, we sacrifice the 'unforced rhythms of grace'[25] for a draining and damaging 'cycle of grief', in which busyness is deemed necessary in order to earn acceptance. In that kind of distorted and destructive version of the 'cycle of grace' modelled by Christ,[26] respect and achievement are viewed as necessary for the self-esteem we crave. The cycle of grace crunches into reverse gear when, whether subconsciously or unconsciously, we embrace the cruel lie: 'What better evidence of our indispensability and significance than a relentless whirl of activity?'

The writings of Henri Nouwen, the Dutch Catholic priest and professor, have crossed all theological and denominational boundaries as they highlight the vital importance of embracing our fundamental identity as people who are loved by God. It sounds so simple and yet our difficulty in holding on to and living from our essential 'belovedness' is one of the greatest challenges of being disciples of Jesus Christ. Once again, to

---

23 Mark 1:11.
24 1 John 4:19.
25 Matthew 11:30 (MSG).
26 For a simple explanation of the insights of clinical psychologist Dr Frank Lake in this regard, see Aisthorpe, *The Invisible Church*, pp. 158–9.

hark back to an earlier chapter ... who we think we are really matters.

In the words of Nouwen, 'When you lose touch with your chosenness, you expose yourself to the temptation of self-rejection, and that temptation undermines the possibility of ever growing as the beloved.'[27] That loss of connection with our fundamental Christian identity is at the root of much well-intended but fruitless busyness because it is at the core of what it means to be joined 'in Christ'. As Jesus explained, 'When you're joined with me and I with you, the relation intimate and organic, the harvest is sure to be abundant. Separated, you can't produce a thing.'[28] Some may baulk at the idea of 'chosenness'. It can sound exclusive and, in an era when inclusiveness is highly valued and rightly so, the suggestion that one is 'chosen' might seem repellent if it is taken to imply that others are not chosen. However, part of the wonder of faith in Christ is that as we grow in the knowledge of our own chosenness, our awareness of the chosenness of others deepens. Far from engendering a sense of self-superiority or a devaluing of others, the opposite occurs.

As one root cause of busyness takes us into the profoundest depths of our personal and corporate spirituality, another takes us to what appears to be mundane and concrete: our diaries! While Peterson's first reason is 'I am busy because I am vain', the second is 'I am busy because I am lazy'. This second confession is not about the behaviour of the 'sluggard' so thoroughly denounced in the book of Proverbs,[29] but is rather about being too idle to take control of our own use of time. Perhaps there is nothing that is distributed with such utter equality and with such absolute limits as time. The president of a superpower gets no additional measure; the most materially poor receives the same daily, weekly and monthly allowance. If anything highlights the fact that we are all equal before God, it is his distribution of time. Peterson's point is that if we are to be people

---

27 Nouwen, H., 1992, *Life of the Beloved*, London: Hodder and Stoughton, p. 56.

28 John 15:5 (MSG).

29 Proverbs 6:6–9; 15:19; 19:24; 21:25 and that is just for starters.

whose values and priorities are reflected in how we live, then we must be proactive in managing our time. That will include ensuring that the most important is not overwhelmed by the urgent. For many of us it will involve developing a gracious, but robust, way of saying no. Together, these temptations to pack our days with eye-catching activity on the one hand and cave in to every expectation and request on the other, lock us into a spiral of conspicuous busyness. They are a recipe for burnout and an effective means of thwarting a prayerful focus on our actual calling; indeed, together they mount a lethal attack on both prayer and focus.

A peek below the surface of much ecclesiastical busyness exposes well-intentioned, but misguided, striving on behalf of God. What appears to be passionate Christian service, an earnest and eager desire to make a difference, easily strays into what Hilary of Tours called *irreligiosa sollicitudo pro Deo*, 'a blasphemous anxiety to do God's work for him'. Living in a nation shaped by free market economics, our working lives often involve the fierce leveraging of 'human capital', a motivating, urging and squeezing of the maximum possible output from people in order to get ahead of the competition. Where this particular invasive species has taken root, we need to rediscover the beauty of the Sabbath principle and remind ourselves that trust in God leads to a place of rest. As in other areas of life, without a clear counter-narrative, church life mirrors the prevailing culture. In the contemporary West, capitalism reigns and a person's achievement is judged on acquisitive success, but the Scriptures offer a radical alternative. At the heart of the Hebrew Bible, we read that, 'It is in vain that you rise up early and go late to rest, eating the bread of anxious toil; for he gives sleep to his beloved.'[30] Coming immediately after a warning against the futility of labour that is not guided and empowered by the Lord ('Unless the Lord builds the house ...'), and set in the middle of the Song of Ascents, these are the words of a communal hymn, to be sung during the journey up to Jerusalem for the pilgrim festivals of Passover, Pentecost and Tabernacles. They are a recurring reminder of the stupidity of exchanging

---

30 Psalm 127:2.

the gift of trust and rest for anxiety and exhaustion. In the New Testament, Jesus' appeal to examples in nature, to ravens and lilies and wild grasses, likewise highlights the senselessness of self-directed striving and the illogicality of anxiety.

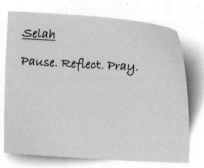

Selah

Pause. Reflect. Pray.

Work is good. In the creation narrative it predates the Fall. Workaholism and constant busyness are not good. If rewilding is to occur we need to learn to listen to and trust God. If we want to listen, we will need to uproot the invasive species of busyness. When a bishop confessed to Mother Teresa, 'I am so busy, that I hardly have time to pray,' she replied, 'If you are too busy to pray, you are too busy!' If we are looking to gauge how busy is too busy, we need look no further.

Tackling the reign of fear

In the north east of Scotland we are waging war on one particular invasive species. They are undeniably beautiful creatures, but rarely seen. Even the most avid wildlife watchers seldom, if ever, see one of these elusive creatures and yet their damage to other species is legendary. The American mink is an opportunistic predator, often killing more than they require for food. Since spreading throughout Scotland after their escape from fur farms in the latter half of the last century, mink have had a devastating effect on ground nesting birds and water vole populations. This semi-aquatic mammal, previously bred for its lush brown fur, terrorises both freshwater and saltwater habitats, following rivers and burns, wreaking havoc along coastlines and around the shores of lochs. We don't see them, but we can observe their impact, which is seen in the paucity of what is left behind. Their legacy is devastated populations of other creatures and diminished biodiversity.

Fortunately for those involved in the Scottish Invasive Species Initiative, the mink's elusiveness is matched by their inquisitiveness. They are one of nature's nosy parkers and experiments have shown that when a small tunnel is mounted on a raft at the edge of water, they cannot resist investigating. Inside each tunnel is a patch of soft clay, on which any creature that passes will leave its paw prints. Where the tell-tale tracks of mink are discovered, a live capture trap is installed in the tunnel, enabling the humane disposal of captured animals. It is a long-term strategy, but gradually a rule of terror is receding.

The Church too is plagued by some reigns of fear. Indeed, some of the invasive species that have wormed their way into the cultures of some church denominations, networks and congregations are different manifestations of fear. Traditionalism (not to be confused with tradition, as will be explained shortly) reveals a fear of change and a veneration of things that have 'always been this way'. The culture of risk aversion that has infested many church institutions hides behind a false notion of tradition, but actually reflects a fear of loss or failure. When John, the apostle, looked back over his many years of following Jesus and pioneering Church, he observed that fear signifies a deficit of love.[31] In common with our tendency towards frenetic activity and the temptation for busyness, when we dig down and expose the roots of other invasive species, we come back to the same underlying issues and the same remedies. Fear entangles and love releases.

Occasionally, in the process of reading and researching, I come across the name of someone who has clearly made enormous contributions to an area of great interest to me, but of whom I had been totally unaware. I have to confess that one such person was Jaroslav Pelikan. Perhaps you are well acquainted with this distinguished Christian historian and theologian, but for those to whom, like me, his name and insights are unknown, let me explain. For much of his life he was an ordained pastor in the Lutheran tradition. His father had been pastor of a Slovak Lutheran Church in Chicago and his paternal grandfather a bishop of the Synod of Evangelical Lutheran

---

31 1 John 4:18.

Churches. These may seem peripheral details, but, as we are discussing matters pertaining to 'tradition' here, they seem pertinent. Later in life he and his wife became members of the Eastern Orthodox Church, but throughout his life he remained passionately ecumenical. For him, brand loyalty had no place in church life, but tradition mattered greatly. Indeed tradition became something of a focus of his exceptional mind (he received honorary degrees from forty-two universities around the world) and generous spirit (it was his earnest longing that churches of all traditions would one day have 'the necessary mixture of charity and sincere effort ... to work toward the time when they all may be one').[32] Invited to give the Jefferson Lecture, the highest honour the US government confers for distinguished intellectual achievement in the humanities, after a lifetime of diligent Christian discipleship and studying ecclesiastical history and the history of theology, he observed: 'Tradition is the living faith of the dead; traditionalism is the dead faith of the living. And, I suppose I should add, it is traditionalism that gives tradition such a bad name.'[33] Please read that again, as Pelikan was saying something of great importance to the Church as it is expressed in the Western world in our time. Tradition is vital; traditional*ism*, the reverence of the current and the resolve to keep things as they are, is toxic.

For many the word 'tradition' conjures up memories of archaic liturgy and hymns with words that are either incomprehensible because of their obscurity or, perhaps worse, rendered hilarious by taking on significantly different meaning in contemporary language. Without further reflection, it is a word that often invokes a sense of sombre solemnity, dismal drudgery, or just plain boredom. In terms of religious faith, it tends to be associated with formality, a characteristic of corporate worship often identified as being unattractive or discouraging by the multitudes who have disengaged from local church congregations in recent years. The *Investigating the Invisible*

---

32 Pelikan, Jaroslav, 2005, 'The Great Unifier', 4 April, *The New York Times* (accessed 17.07.2019).

33 Pelikan, Jaroslav, 1984, *The Vindication of Tradition*, Newhaven, CT: Yale University Press, p. 65.

Church study[34] discovered that while 11 per cent had found the congregations they had attended too informal, nearly four times that number had walked away from an experience of church that had been 'too formal'. However, as implied by Pelikan's carefully chosen terminology of 'living faith', tradition is not shorthand for ancient rituals or practices, long past their 'best before' date, seemingly stuck in a time-warp. Indeed, to be faithful as followers of Christ *requires* that we interact with tradition, that we learn from and build on what is valuable from our forebears. As we engage with how our sisters and brothers in past generations have encountered and responded to God's love and action, we reflect and become part of tradition.

Not only does traditionalism 'give tradition a bad name', it operates by disguising itself as tradition. I remember when my brother first began work in a bank in the 1980s, he needed to learn how to distinguish genuine currency from counterfeit. He was not trained to recognise the features of every different forgery. Rather, he learned to recognise the hallmarks of the real thing. The best defence against traditionalism is a well-developed love of tradition, the living faith of the dead.

The writer of Psalm 78 was describing the dynamic processes of tradition when he wrote:

My people, hear my teaching;
　　listen to the words of my mouth.
I will open my mouth with a parable;
　　I will utter hidden things, things from of old –
things we have heard and known,
　　things our ancestors have told us.
We will not hide them from their descendants;
　　we will tell the next generation
the praiseworthy deeds of the Lord,
　　his power, and the wonders he has done.[35]

---

34 Aisthorpe, S., 2014, 'A survey of Christians in the Highlands and Islands who are not part of a church congregation', *Rural Theology*, November 12(2), pp. 83–95.

35 Psalm 78:1–4 (NIV).

The psalmist knew what it meant to be a link in the chain of faith history. He put immense value on being the recipient of wisdom and insight from previous generations. Likewise, he appreciated that, included with the great blessings inherited, there was a profound responsibility to not just pass on history in a faithful fashion, but to enact his part of the ongoing saga of Yahweh's walking with and shaping of his people. The psalmist tells us about how his ancestors were loved and changed by God; he recognises his own life as being a crucible for the same processes at work; his psalm then becomes what one commentator has described as 'a drama that calls for response from the congregation'.[36] So, in the Christian Way, tradition refers to the wondrous continuity of God's redemptive activity in the lives of his people, the golden thread of divine grace that runs through history and eternity.

A tradition of risk that counters fear

In this chapter we have already found wisdom for our postmodern world in the words of the ancient epistle we call the Letter to the Hebrews. But we should note that when the writer of that letter penned his exhortation 'to fix our eyes on Jesus' and 'to throw off everything that hinders and the sin that so easily entangles' he did so immediately after reminding them of the 'great cloud of witnesses' that 'surround' his readers. This is what Dr Pelikan had in mind when he described 'tradition' as 'the living faith of the dead'. It is not, as I have sometimes heard preached, that the heroes of the biblical record listed in Hebrews 11 are looking down from heaven, watching our progress and cheering us on towards the finishing line. Rather, it is that their lives bear witness to us of God's faithfulness; the fact that 'by faith' they persevered against all the odds and remained faithful in the face of intense opposition speaks words of encouragement and exhortation across the intervening centuries. This is tradition at work: all of those listed in

---

36 Brueggemann, W. and W. Bellinger, 2019, *Psalms*, Cambridge: Cambridge University Press, p. 341.

that roll call of the faithful inherited testimony to God's faithfulness, they applied what they understood of God's call in their own context, and now their faithfulness speaks to us.

G. K. Chesterton, the philosopher-theologian with a gift for composing memorable proverbs and allegories, described tradition as 'the democracy of the dead'. In *Orthodoxy*, his exploration of the foundations and essence of the Christian faith, he explains that, just as democracy as a political system gives a voice to everyone regardless of their social standing, so tradition ensures that the wisdom of those who are no longer alive continues to have influence: 'democrats object to men being disqualified by the accident of birth; tradition objects to their being disqualified by the accident of death'.[37] Both Pelikan and Chesterton highlight the importance and value of tradition. When we fail to pay attention to the prophetic influence of tradition, we discard the wealth of past wisdom of multiple generations and muddle through with whatever minimal resources are available here and now in this particular cultural moment in eternity. As Chesterton put it, 'Tradition refuses to submit to the small and arrogant oligarchy of those who merely happen to be walking about.'[38] Tradition is protection against what has been called the 'narcissism of now', defence from a focus on the here and now with no regard for centuries of accumulated wisdom. Tradition anchors us in truth; traditionalism anchors us to the spot, whereas we need to always be on the move: 'A church which pitches its tents without constantly looking out for new horizons, which does not continually strike camp, is being untrue to its calling … [We must] play down our longing for certainty, accept what is risky, and live by improvisation and experiment.'[39]

Before the potent forces within nature can be released in rewilding, the environment needs to be liberated from the destructive stranglehold of invasive species. If the transformative power at the heart of the Church is to be unleashed and

---

37 Chesterton, G. K., *Orthodoxy*, chapter 4, www.gkc.org.uk/gkc/books/orthodoxy/ch4.html (original work published 1908).

38 Chesterton, G. K., 2012, *Orthodoxy*, Simon & Brown, pp. 27–39.

39 Küng, H., 1967, *The Church*, London: Burns and Oates, pp. 130–1.

its purpose fulfilled, we need to stop seeking to convince one another that activity is in and of itself worthwhile. Likewise, if our actions are to be in step with what the Spirit is doing, we must reject the cult of busyness and relearn a balance of contemplation and action. In these challenging times for church institutions there is much talk of risk-taking, courageous creativity and innovation, but unless the fear at the heart of our risk averse cultures is uprooted, our well-intentioned rhetoric will remain as only that.

The Australian missiologists Frost and Hirsch assert that the Church 'should be one of the most adventurous places on earth – the locus of all quest, the highly adaptive Jesus community at the very forefront of what God is doing in the world',[40] but let's be honest and admit that many of the congregations and organisations that own the name 'church' are deeply risk averse by nature. One could almost believe that the Great Commission stated something along the lines of 'Stay and keep things going'. The source of *that* command is tradition*alism*, whereas our traditions encourage risk as an essential element of good stewardship. In what we often call the Parable of the Talents (talents as in a measure of weight, which later became a monetary unit, not talents as in human skills and abilities),[41] the focus is on risk and faithfulness. The most cautious servant, the one whose focus is on carefully retaining what is already in hand, is viewed as unfaithful. Those who took risks are commended.

The extermination of the American mink and the Himalayan balsam began with a change of perception. When a mink was no longer seen as a furry friend, but a ruthless killer, their culling became acceptable; when a stand of balsam was not appreciated as an attractive flower, but began to be recognised as an invasive pest, their elimination became an acceptable cause. My personal reflections on what might constitute 'invasive species' for the Church began with an extensive list, but

---

40 Frost, M. and A. Hirsch, 2011, *The Faith of Leap: Embracing a Theology of Risk, Adventure and Courage*, Grand Rapids, MI: Baker, p. 24.

41 Matthew 25:14–30.

boiled down to three elements of our church cultures. Like the uprooting and clearing of balsam, releasing their grip is a long-term undertaking, one that will lead to transformation, and begins with a change of mind.

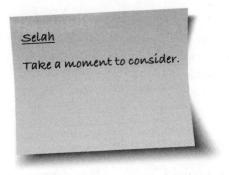

Selah

Take a moment to consider.

HOPE: From Lament to Trust

'I am about to do a new thing; now it springs forth,
do you not perceive it? I will make a way in the
wilderness and rivers in the desert.'
Isaiah 43:19

From barrenness to flourishing

In May 1980, Mount St Helens, a long-dormant volcano in the US state of Washington, exploded with devastating power. In the moments of extreme violence that followed, a 300-mile-an-hour blast of superheated air and debris flattened the surrounding old growth forest. The upper 400 metres of the mountain was blasted away. Fire and molten rock rained down. Within minutes a dense column of ash punched 25,000 metres into the sky and began to drift to earth over several surrounding states. More than 230 square miles of forest, lakes, rivers and meadow was devastated. One of the first ecologists to visit the area following the eruption, Professor Virginia Dale, reported a scene of utter destruction and barrenness: 'It gave the impression of total lifelessness.'[1]

However, over the years that followed, as Dale and her colleagues monitored those apparently sterile pumice slopes, they witnessed the gradual, but resolute, return of life. Dale's team has recorded more than 150 species of wildflowers, shrubs and trees. Species of conifer like the western hemlock and Pacific silver fir that orthodox ecology said should not be

---

1 Williams, D., 2005, 'Rising from the ashes', *Smithsonian Magazine*, May, www.smithsonianmag.com/history/rising-from-the-ashes-770471 81/ (accessed 20.01.20).

there, trees that scientists had believed required generations of the soil-developing activities of other plants, are back.

Two years after the eruption, a Forest Service ecologist, Charlie Crisafulli, was flying over an area that had been decimated by torrents of superheated air, gases and carpeted in ash, when he spotted a splash of colour. On landing the helicopter nearby, he discovered a small cluster of *prairie lupine*. It was a surprise discovery on several counts. These lupines are not considered a 'pioneer species', the kind of hardy plants that are the first to colonise environments where natural processes have been disrupted. They are a ground-hugging, slow-spreading plant, with heavy seeds that are not easily dispersed by wind. However, as a member of the pea family, they have the capacity to get the nitrogen they need from bacteria that live on their roots. Over the following years Crisafulli and colleagues kept watch. Four years later, within a 200-square-yard study area around that first pioneering plant, he counted 16,000 lupines. After a further three years that number had doubled.

Wind almost certainly played a key role in the return of life to barren slopes, blowing in spiders, insects and seeds from nearby undisturbed areas. The *western pearly everlasting*, a flowering perennial plant in the sunflower family with seeds that are easily carried by wind, was an early pioneer. Other species probably regenerated from root fragments, remnants of the old landscape known as 'biological legacies'.[2] Following the regeneration of plant life, ground squirrels, mice and shrews began to return, each accelerating the area's recovery by collecting and storing seeds, burrowing through soil and luring predators such as raptors and weasels back into the ecosystem. Today, dense thickets of alders and willows, many three to five metres tall, line the banks of streams that cross the pumice plain below the peak. A herd of elks graze the area.

---

2 Dale, Virginia, Frederick J. Swanson, and Charles M. Crisafulli (eds), 2005, *Ecological Responses to the 1980 Eruption of Mount St. Helens*, New York, NY: Springer, www.fs.fed.us/pnw/pubs/journals/pnw_2005_dale003.pdf (accessed 20.01.2020).

The air is full of birdsong. In what is the blink of an eye in the history of landscape, life has bounced back.

At the heart of the natural world are potent forces for regeneration and thriving. Most of the landscape we see around us is the outcome of humankind constraining and managing those forces. Neatly manicured lawns and fields of a single species of wheat or vegetable testify to humankind's power to exert our will upon the environment, but, when given the chance, biodiversity returns as biotic potential kicks in. Even in situations of apparent sterility and desolation, a powerful potential for rebirth and renewal lurks below the surface.

Creation on tiptoe

When Paul was writing to the emerging churches in Rome, he painted a vivid word-picture of this eager desire in God's creation, a yearning, a longing for regeneration. The J. B. Phillips translation speaks of 'The whole creation ... on tiptoe';[3] *The Message* evokes an image of creation straining at the leash or champing at the bit: 'Everything in creation is being more or less held back. God reins it in until both creation and all the creatures are ready and can be released at the same moment into the glorious times ahead.'[4] Paul instructed his readers to recognise signs of present-day frustration, waiting and pain in the natural world that point towards a glorious future when what is currently hidden 'will be revealed' (v.18) and what is currently held back will be 'set free' (v.21). The subject of the eager anticipation he depicts comes into focus with the word 'hope'. As one New Testament scholar observes, 'The word "hope" is the pivot on which Paul turns from the past to the future of creation.'[5] Within the whole of creation, and within God's children in particular, there is a mounting anticipation and a deepening joy, as we wait for the fulfilment of God's

---

3 Romans 8:19 (Phillips).
4 Romans 8:18–21 (MSG).
5 Stott, J., 2007, *The Message of Romans*, London: IVP, p. 239.

purposes, the consummation of the kingdom, the ultimate regeneration. We see signs of the kingdom now, the Church among them, but they are an inkling of what we hope for. Where we witness love and justice we rejoice and are encouraged that there is much more to come.

Paul's is just one voice among a choir of Spirit-inspired writers who all caught fleeting glimpses of an inexpressible future glory. Old Testament authors, especially in Psalms and Isaiah, depicted the promised future in terms of a superabundance in biodiversity and environmental harmony;[6] Jesus pointed to a 'renewal of all things';[7] Paul expounded the concepts of reconciliation and liberation;[8] John conveyed a vivid image of a new heaven and earth in which current barriers will disappear and the causes of present suffering will no longer exist;[9] Peter passionately believed that the visions of generations of prophets pointed to a 'time of universal restoration'.[10] The language and imagery differ, but what is consistent is a future that is so magnificent as to defy description. When Martin Luther King referred to the long arc of the moral universe bending towards justice[11] he was highlighting one aspect of this irrevocable movement towards the total regeneration of creation.

Rewilding recognises that when nature is unleashed there is a powerful innate tendency towards biodiversity and abundance. Interventions to reintroduce missing species and remove invasive species are ways of removing obstructions, of lending a hand and speeding the process. As part of creation we can act in ways that facilitate and accelerate the movement towards environmental health or we can interfere in ways that hinder

---

6 For example, Isaiah 11:6–9; Isaiah 32:16–20; Isaiah 35.

7 Matthew 19:28.

8 Colossians 1:20; Ephesians 1:10.

9 Revelation 21—22.

10 Acts 3:21.

11 Martin Luther King Jr (1929–68), Christian minister and prominent activist in the American Civil Rights Movement, used variations of the phrase 'the arc of the moral universe is long, but it bends toward justice' in several speeches. It was a phrase first coined by nineteenth-century clergyman Theodore Parker.

and obstruct. We cannot drive the process, but we can seek to be in step or at least to not get in the way. Likewise, as followers of Jesus, we have a responsibility to live in harmony with the trajectory of God's purpose or at least to avoid being obstacles. In recent decades a renewed theology of mission has highlighted the need for the Church to see its role in terms of discerning God's activity and participating *with* God. The idea of *missio Dei*, literally 'the sending of God', sees the Church as being an important agent in God's mission, but emphasises the primacy of God's initiative. In contrast with a *missio ecclesiae* perspective that sees the 'mission of the Church' in terms of certain preconceived roles, when we understand ourselves through the lens of *missio Dei*: 'It is not the church of God that has a mission in the world, but the God of mission who has a church in the world.'[12] Such a viewpoint sees the Church's involvement in mission as connecting with what God is already doing. To view the Church through the lens of *missio Dei* is to find its responsibility as being, in the words of previous archbishop Rowan Williams, 'finding out what God is doing and joining in'.[13]

Once again we find that who we think we are is really important. We are sent people. To say 'yes' to Jesus' invitation to 'follow me' leads to the further summons to go: 'As the Father has sent me, so I send you.'[14] Our purpose in the world is a continuation of what Jesus began: 'The Church is sent into the world to continue that which he came to do, in the power of the Spirit, reconciling people to God.'[15] To be the body of Christ, to be able to faithfully continue what he has started, requires that we grow in character in ways that reflect his

---

12 Dearborn, T., 1997, *Beyond Duty: A Passion for Christ, a Heart for Mission*, MARC, p. 2.

13 'Archbishop's Presidential Address – General Synod, York, July 2003', http://aoc2013.brix.fatbeehive.com/articles.php/1826/archbishops-presidential-address-general-synod-york-july-2003 (accessed 27.01.2020).

14 John 20:21.

15 Newbigin, L., 1989, *The Gospel in a Pluralist Society*, Grand Rapids, MI: Eerdmans, p. 230.

nature. If we are to love others 'as Christ loved' we need *that* kind of love. The powerful inner urge that Paul parallels with nature's innate urge for regeneration is love: love for God and love for others. The Church, in all its diverse expressions, must be a means of growing in love and expressing that love. As Brian McLaren puts it, 'the church must be above all a school of love. If it's not that, it's nothing.'[16]

Selah

Take a minute to reflect?

From angst to hope

As I write this final chapter, political and business leaders have been gathering at the World Economic Forum in Davos. US President Donald Trump's keynote speech urged business leaders to stop listening to the warnings of environmental crisis from 'prophets of doom'. Seventeen-year-old Swedish activist Greta Thunberg, speaking at the same event, blasted politicians and CEOs for their inaction and failure to take seriously the signs of environmental catastrophe. Meanwhile the term 'eco-anxiety' has entered our vocabulary. The protest group Extinction Rebellion have begun holding 'grief-tending workshops'. As current trends suggest that climate breakdown and mass extinctions could trigger the collapse of our civilisation, it is hardly surprising that some people are experiencing a welling up of despair that is undermining their mental well-being. At a recent gathering of psychotherapists to discuss how best to manage the fear that people are experiencing over our impact on the planet, Sarah Niblock, the CEO of the UK Council for Psychotherapy, explained that '[Eco-anxiety] is not an illness

---

16 McLaren, B., 2011, *A New Kind of Christianity*, London: Hodder and Stoughton, pp. 170–1.

or disorder, it's a perfectly normal and healthy reaction'.[17] While fear may be a normal response, it may not be helpful; the danger is that, rather than motivating radical change, it can lead to paralysis, a sense that the challenges are too big and beyond our hoping. In the midst of what the United Nations (UN) has identified as 'the defining crisis of our time',[18] there is an urgent and vital need for hope. The future of our planet depends on us being concerned enough to take drastic action and not so terrified that we are petrified into inaction. We need to believe the message of UN Secretary-General António Guterres, 'the climate emergency is a race we are losing, but it is a race we can win',[19] and see examples and hear stories that give us hope. Accounts of rewilding, small and local, extensive and ambitious, demonstrate the capacity of nature to bounce back. Alone, it is not the answer to the global emergency, but as well as the benefits it brings to the ecosystems that are allowed to thrive, it is a source of hope.

For those whose Christian faith has been tightly intertwined with church institutions, the dramatic decline of those organisations can be a source of 'ecclesia-anxiety' just as threatening to healthy faith and purposeful change of perspective as extreme eco-anxiety. Those who remain within declining institutions may adopt a kind of remnant theology, viewing the mass exodus of recent years as a spiritual pruning; or they may fall prey to a harmful cynicism, owning many of the same perspectives of those who have disengaged, but remaining in a congregation out of habit. Some draw hope from the Church as a whole and find rich opportunities for faithful Christian living in the context of a waning denomination, group or congregation. Others,

---

17 Sarchet, P., 2019, 'Stressed about climate change?', *New Scientist*, October, www.newscientist.com/article/2220561-stressed-about-climate-change-eight-tips-for-managing-eco-anxiety/ (accessed 31.01.2020).

18 United Nations, 'The Climate Crisis – a race we can win', *United Nations*, www.un.org/en/un75/climate-crisis-race-we-can-win (accessed 02.03.2020).

19 António Guterres's remarks at 2019 Climate Action Summit, 23 September 2019, www.un.org/sg/en/content/sg/speeches/2019-09-23/remarks-2019-climate-action-summit (accessed 27.01.2020).

often on or beyond the edge of church institutions, find that following Jesus draws them into proximity with others and find themselves at the nucleus of one of the grassroots communities of faith that are emerging from the post-Christendom wilderness.

From anguish to outcry

I was in my mid-twenties when I first felt *compelled* to pray. At that time I was obsessed with climbing, had minimal knowledge of Jesus and no interest in Christian faith. It was early January and I was clinging to a frozen waterfall in Norway. Daylight was fading, my strength was failing, and on the final vertical sweep of ice I became as frozen as the icy cascade itself. Exhausted, petrified, contemplating the horrific consequences of the bone-shattering plunge that now seemed inevitable, I began to pray. It began as a simple, silent cry of desperation: 'Help! HELP! Please, please get me out of here!' As I hung there it occurred to me that I had only two options. I could hang on for a little longer, until, once the last leftovers of strength were gone, I would plummet to my death, probably taking my partner with me. Alternatively, if I had even an ounce of trust in the One to whom I had just found myself praying, I could put that flicker of faith into action by pressing on. Over the next few minutes, with a precision and strength that I knew were well beyond my own capacities to marshal, I picked and kicked my way up that final wall of ice. With each movement I implored God to guide the swing of my ice axe or direct the placing of my crampons. As I heaved my body over the final icy bulge, I did not undergo a miraculous conversion, but that experience did prompt the beginning of an intentional search to understand what happened in those intense few minutes, drawn taut between life and death – a search that led to me embracing the Christian faith a few months later.

Prayer is first and foremost a gift of grace, an undeserved and sometimes unrequested gift of communication. What I learned later is that, when words will not come, when we have no idea how to pray, when we feel unable to muster Godward thoughts, the Spirit 'intercedes'. He intervenes on our behalf, becomes our intermediary, and does that which we are unable to do. He is, after all, our 'helper' or 'advocate', the one sent to teach us.[20] He stirs in us the desire to pray and guides our prayers. When we are tongue-tied, when adequate language eludes us, the Helper prays on our behalf. I'm sure that I am not alone in having 'Help' as the first word in my prayer vocabulary. Other commonplace spontaneous prayer outbursts are expressions of gratitude or awe or something along the lines of 'How long, O Lord?'

How long? How long? How long? How long? Yes, four times the writer of the outpouring of the lament that is Psalm 13 cries out that heart-rending question. When we turn to the very heart of our Bibles, to the magnificent book of Psalms, what are we usually searching for or expecting? A rousing call to worship perhaps? There are certainly plenty of those: 'Shout for joy to the Lord, all the earth. Worship the Lord with gladness; come before him with joyful songs.'[21] Or might we be looking for words of soul-warming assurance? Those too are in plentiful supply: 'The Lord is my shepherd, I lack nothing. He makes me lie down in green pastures, he leads me beside quiet waters, he refreshes my soul.'[22] Whatever we seek and find in the psalms, however, unless we are exceptionally precise in our cherry picking, we cannot avoid bumping into the kinds of outpouring of complaint and grief that we find in Psalm 13. 'How long, O Lord?'

Within the Psalter there are torrents of individual angst and objection; there are copious communal expressions of torment and protest. The authors of these hymns and poems had a faith that involved wrestling, weeping and objecting. Their faith was no stiff-upper-lipped stoicism. It was more like a full-on, no-holds-barred grappling with the Almighty. If the decisions about the biblical canon were made with the feel-good culture of the twenty-first century in mind, one cannot help imagin-

20 John 14:26.
21 Psalm 100.
22 Psalm 23.

ing that nearly half of the psalms would have been extensively redacted by some well-meaning spin doctors, Job would have been carefully censored, and the proposal for the exclusion of the book of Lamentations in total would have won unanimous support.

We live at a time of impoverished spirituality. Reflecting on the Christian response to suffering, Bible scholar D. A. Carson bemoans the dearth of healthy lament in Western spirituality. In contrast to the Godward complaint and open weeping of the psalms, he observes that, 'where faith triumphs in adversity, we expect it to be manifest in unmoved resignation, and where faith fails the failure is displayed in doubt that questions the integrity and possibly even the existence of God'.[23]

We are indebted to the authors and collectors of the Hebrew Scriptures for their authenticity, ruthless honesty and integrity. While collections of both traditional hymns and modern worship songs often leave us mute in the face of suffering and injustice, we can still turn to the psalms. In a recent tweet, American singer-songwriter Michael Gungor made the observation that while the 150 psalms include between sixty and seventy laments, when he looked at the top 150 most often used Christians hymns and songs as recorded by Christian Copyright Licensing International (CCLI), there was not a single lament. However, it is interesting to note that where Christians are wrestling with the challenges confronting both the natural environment and the Church, the ancient genre of lament is providing a vocabulary for a contemporary and fresh response.[24]

Despite their ancient origins and the fact that some of their Hebrew poetic style is inevitably lost in translation, the psalms *speak* to us. They speak of our almighty creator and sustainer, but they also give us a language with which we can speak *with*

---

23 Carson, D., 2006, *How Long, O Lord?: Reflections on Suffering and Evil*, Grand Rapids, MI: Baker Academic, p. 67.

24 An example would be the work of David Benjamin Blower, co-host of Nomad, a podcast and online community encouraging those 'stumbling through the post-Christendom wilderness, looking for signs of hope': www.nomadpodcast.co.uk.

him. While the psalms contain words *from* God and *about* God, they also include words *to* God. Words and phrases that were penned more than five centuries before the birth of Jesus Christ continue to give us a vocabulary of praise, grief, doubt, trust, anger, thanksgiving, and much more. When we mess up big time it's hard to find more apt and expressive phrases of wholehearted confession and of intense longing for forgiveness than the words of David following his adultery with Bathsheba and murder of Uriah.[25] When anxiety threatens to overwhelm us, the reminder that 'God is our refuge and strength, an ever-present help in trouble' and the invitation 'Be still, and know that I am God'[26] have a remarkable power to ground us in the love of an omnipotent provider. When low mood looms and the black dog of depression skulks in the shadows, some of those psalms attributed to sons of Korah offer healing balm.[27]

When leading retreats over the years I have sometimes invited people to 'meet themselves in the psalms', to find a psalm that resonates with their current situation or reflects the way they currently feel. Then, through reflecting on that psalm and how it speaks to their own circumstances, they create their own psalm. Without fail people encounter words and phrases that express their own emotions and experiences and provide them with a vocabulary of prayer and worship. It is notable how, time and again, people are surprised by the prevalence of lament and find through that particular genre a means to explore and process sources of disappointment and heartache.

The trajectory of hope

What differentiates lament from common or garden moaning is its Godward orientation and the consequent transformation. Academics observe that a characteristic of lament as a genre in the Bible is the movement from 'plea to praise': 'The wonder

---

25 Psalm 51.
26 Psalm 46.
27 Psalms 42, 44—49, 84, 85, 87 and 88.

of these prayers is that the prayers *move*, so that everything is different at the end from what it was at the beginning.'[28] On one level this 'move' takes place within the literary form, it is a rhetorical movement. However, the poetry reflects the reality of experience, the radical change of perspective that God brings. These texts are literary, historical, theological, but also more. Dietrich Bonhoeffer, a man who was well acquainted with persecution and suffering, considered the psalms to be 'The Prayer Book of the Bible' and observed that biblical lamentation, far from being an outlet, is a gateway: 'Praying certainly does not mean simply pouring out one's heart. It means, rather, finding the way to and speaking with God, whether the heart is full or empty.'[29]

In the early months of shaping this book, I certainly didn't expect to be writing about lament. However, when we consider anything that evokes heartfelt distress, whether well-justified concerns for the natural environment, for impoverished church, or for anything else, the biblical pattern of lament offers a pathway from honest outcry to trust in God and hope. Little did I know it when I expressed my desperation on the Norwegian icefall, but the path from outcry to faith is something of a shortcut. The outcry of lament has the essence of faith within it. Perhaps the fact that a four-fold 'How long, Lord' should lead in a few short verses to the profound declaration of faith, 'I trust in your unfailing love',[30] is not so surprising. As Paul Bradbury has explained: 'Lament is God's gift to us to enable fierce and *faithful* honesty in the context of suffering. The complaint within lament is not a precursor to faith; *it is faith*.'[31]

Where do you long to see rewilding by God? Is there a situation in which you long for God's Spirit to bring new life?

---

28 Brueggemann, W. and W. Bellinger, 2019, *Psalms*, Cambridge: Cambridge University Press, p. 77.

29 Bonhoeffer, D., 2005, *Life Together / Prayerbook of the Bible (DBW, 5)*, G. B. Kelly (ed.), trans. D. W. Bloesch and J. H. Burtness; Minneapolis, MN: Fortress Press, p. 155.

30 Psalm 13:5 (NIV).

31 Bradbury, P., 2019, *Home By Another Route*, Abingdon: Bible Reading Fellowship, p. 41.

Has God put a concern in your heart for particular people and places? Nehemiah, deeply moved by the devastating news that the Jewish remnant in Jerusalem were in 'great trouble and disgrace',[32] travelled to the city and inspected the ruined walls.[33] It was more than an exercise in quantity surveying; as Nehemiah toured the derelict walls, he was testing what God had put in his heart and discerning what his next steps should be. In the case of Ezekiel, he was led 'back and forth'[34] among the bones of a valley through some kind of prayer encounter or vision, but Nehemiah's was a physical prayer walk, under the cover of darkness, with a few trusted others. Whether through a physical walk or in prayerful contemplation, whether alone or with trusted others, begin to express the troubles or desires in your heart as lamentation. Peter's direction, 'Cast all your anxiety on him because he cares for you',[35] popular on fridge magnets and greeting cards, is in fact a quote from a classic psalm of lament that begins with a no-holds-barred outpouring of distress.[36] The term 'cast' suggests the heaving and rolling motion of loading a heavy burden on to the back of a camel. The burden is not shared; it is transferred from one to another, totally. Peter's instruction is part of his teaching on humility. The casting of our burdens is the means by which we humble ourselves, as we admit what is outside our control and beyond our capabilities. Be 'honest to God', allow your emotions to surface and share them openly. Let your complaints and concerns flow and resist being hurried into anything else; be reassured this is a legitimate expression of faith.

When the burden is no longer ours, the time is right for the journey of lamentation to move from distress to intercession. Not a shopping list or a wish list. Not a flexing of spiritual muscle. It is in the place of humility, which we encounter in the midst of lamentation, that we understand and experience what Paul recorded: '... the Spirit helps us in our weakness; for we

---

32 Nehemiah 1:3 (NIV).
33 Nehemiah 2:13ff.
34 Ezekiel 37:2.
35 1 Peter 5:7.
36 Psalm 55:22.

do not know how to pray as we ought, but the Spirit himself intercedes for us with sighs too deep for words'.[37] Yes, prayer is a discipline, but it is first and foremost a gift of grace. And, when words will not come, when we have no idea how to pray, when we feel unable to muster Godward thoughts, the Spirit 'intercedes'. He intervenes on our behalf, becomes our intermediary, does that which we are unable to do and moves us along the trajectory of hope.

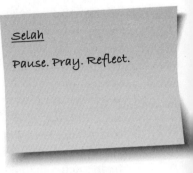

Selah

Pause. Pray. Reflect.

From love to innovation

It is from this place of Spirit-inspired hope that authentic mission springs and grows. Too often, what is encouraged and practised by church institutions in the name of 'mission' is actually a thinly concealed recruitment drive, motivated by a desire to boost numbers and perpetuate a particular congregation or group. The results of such attempts at church conscription usually reflect the fact that most people can distinguish between authentic love and just drumming up support. In the dozens of accounts of Christians who are no longer engaged with church congregations, love is the oft-stated reason for why they were drawn to the Christian faith in the first place and its lack is at least part of their reason for disengagement. One correspondent explained how a congregation they encountered 'won me over ... with its love and power when I had barriers against organised religion a mile high – it smashed them down'.[38] Another spoke of feeling 'embarrassed – yeah, even ashamed' because of the way a congregation was experienced by his friends, neighbours and work colleagues as 'judgemen-

---

37 Romans 8:26 (RSV).

38 Aisthorpe, S., 2016, *The Invisible Church: Learning from the Experiences of Churchless Christians*, Edinburgh: Saint Andrew Press, p. 69.

tal, negative – yeah, just having nothing positive to say to the people round about'.[39] I'll never forget the impassioned outburst of one interviewee who, towards the end of her lengthy and intense account, had a realisation about the vital place of love in the Church: 'I'm really – stopping myself because I can just hear myself what I've said, that the love – is because there isn't love. It's actually because there isn't, that people are sitting outside the Church. Do you know, I actually realised that is it. I'm feeling it in my heart, because I'm saying it out loud. I hadn't actually thought it as conclusively as that. There is not the love. In the Church if the love of Christ is really not coming through from top to bottom ... The Church has got to learn to love again – that is it, that – is – it!'[40]

It is as we ask God for more love for those we encounter and find to be our neighbours that missional imagination is triggered and opportunities for expressing the love of Christ emerge. When we read the Gospels we find that God's masterplan for redeeming creation is marked by vulnerability, it is intensely personal, it is enacted through the encounters and words and actions of Jesus and then his followers, each unique and each manifesting love. We too are grafted into that same heritage of loving words and actions. As we open our hearts to God and confess a desire to be drawn into the flow of divine purpose, the love we receive is not a general love for everyone, but a particular love for specific people. Re-envisioning the Church for mission is no more or no less than growing in love. French author Antoine de Saint-Exupéry wrote that, 'If you want to build a ship, don't drum up the men to gather wood, divide the work and give orders. Instead, teach them to yearn for the vast and endless sea.'[41] We might say, 'If you want to

---

39 Aisthorpe, *The Invisible Church*, p. 156.

40 Aisthorpe, *The Invisible Church*, pp. 152–3.

41 While there is no exact match for this statement in the works of de Saint-Exupéry, there is a section in LXXV of *Citadelle* (1948), translated into English as *The Wisdom of the Sands*, in which he writes about a person who wants to build a boat, imparted a love of sailing to a group of people, and the group were motivated to perform the necessary tasks.

rewild the Church, don't promote mission strategy and teach church-planting tactics. Instead, foster a trust in Jesus and nurture a deeper love for those he brings across our path.'

Love for others is a gift from God, one that is willingly given, the fruit of the Spirit's work within us. It is sometimes a choice, a decision to adopt a path that is not our natural inclination, a determination to refuse unloving thoughts. Where love grows there is a desire to *do* something. Love is a noun that longs to be a verb. It needs to find expression. Where love grows, innovation is prompted, as people seek ways to express that love in action. When I reflect on the experience of journeying with congregations and groups as they develop vision for sharing the love of Christ, it seems that signs of rewilding spring up most vigorously not necessarily where a congregation develops an exciting plan for five or ten years, but rather where a culture of experimentation and learning is cultivated, where people are encouraged to use their gifts and given the freedom to try things, where every outcome is seen as a source of valuable learning and discerning what God is doing.

Bold, persistent experimentation

The early 1930s was a desperately challenging time for world leaders, as they wrestled with the ramifications of The Great Depression. On 22 May 1932, the then New York Governor, Franklin D. Roosevelt, gave a rousing speech that became historically significant as the beginning of the future President's New Deal plan: 'The country needs and, unless I mistake its temper, the country demands bold, persistent experimentation. It is common sense to take a method and try it: if it fails, admit it frankly and try another. But above all, try something.'

I am not suggesting a random policy of 'try anything'. Actions need to emerge from prayerful listening, but then need to be seen as the beginning of an ongoing process of discernment through regular review and intentional learning. Over time, routines of repetition are replaced by patterns of iteration. The habit of identifying and developing the gifts of those whom

God brings into the group or congregation undermines any tendency towards clericalism and creates a culture of participation. The practice of observing the responses of individuals and the wider community to initiatives and seeing this in terms of God's mission creates a dynamic learning community.

Many denominations are waking up to the fundamental calling of Christians to a life-long journey of growing in Christ. However, the congregations, groups and networks that comprise the Church are also called to a corporate discipleship. For rewilding to flourish, for genuine participation in the *missio Dei* to take root, a culture of prayerful, Spirit-led innovation, a cycle of holy experimentation, evaluation and learning, needs to be fostered. The Church needs and, unless I mistake its temper, the Church demands bold, persistent experimentation. Try something. Not any old thing, but what is inspired by this Spirit-led journey of lament and prayer. Try something. Then celebrate and build on what goes well. And celebrate too all that does not go as hoped – because it is there we'll find a source of rich learning and a springboard for what comes next.

Encouraging fertile margins

In the countryside of north-western Europe there are few areas of genuine wilderness and even semi-natural habitats are often a small part of a mosaic of cultivated fields and human infrastructures. Outside of northern Scotland and some of the wildest parts of Wales, the best hopes for rewilding in the UK are on a small scale. Increasingly field margins are allowed to be sites of small-scale rewilding. Spurred on by studies that show the long-term benefits to the sustainability of production and encouraged by financial incentives, landowners are leaving hedge-side areas and other strips of land as undisturbed as possible – and, as they do, biodiversity is returning. Insects whose life cycle would be disrupted by the mowing or grazing that takes place in the rest of the field have opportunities to thrive. Even quite narrow strips, freed from fertiliser and insecticide for periods of time, have been shown to boost populations of species decimated by modern land use practices. Voles, harvest mice, barn owls and yellowhammers flourish around these deliberately neglected margins. Farmers have long known that, if productivity is measured in terms of the single crop that is being cultivated, field edges routinely yield up to 25 per cent less than areas in the centre of a field, hence the drive for bigger fields. However, when local biodiversity and the well-being of the whole environment are counted as valuable, areas around the margins become highly valued as the breeding grounds of endangered species, havens for pollinating insects, and vital wildlife corridors, linking woodlands, hedgerows and other areas of 'planned neglect'.[42]

What about the Church? Where are the 'edges' and areas free of control? Dutch Professor Stefan Paas, director of the Centre for Church and Mission in the West (CCMW), argues that both in the history of Christianity in Europe and in the experience of the contemporary Church, 'Renewal comes from the margin, and rarely from the center.'[43] In the case of an agricultural field, it is the fact that areas close to the perimeter escape the full impact of activities designed to maximise the yield of a particular crop that makes them so fruitful for other species. In both field and Church, 'margins' are places characterised by distance from centres of control. Historical denominations tend to have highly developed administrative systems and legal frameworks, and see certain roles and activities as being the preserve of ordained clergy. In these contexts, a culture of clericalism can develop in which clergy are viewed as superior in virtue and wisdom and so-called 'lay people' as somehow lesser. As the current Pope has written, this kind of culture can be fostered and maintained by both ordained or lay, by priests or clergy supposing superiority, or by others assuming and behaving as if ordained persons know best. At the other extreme, many in the so-called 'invisible church' have

---

42 Stoate, C. and colleagues, 2013, *Fields for the Future: The Allerton Project – A Winning Blueprint for Farming, Wildlife and the Environment*, Game Conservancy.

43 Paas, S., 2016, *Church Planting in the Secular West: Learning from the European Experience*, Grand Rapids, MI: Eerdmans, p. 225.

chosen to be at a distance from centres of control. While many seek out informal relationships or networks of accountability, with some aligning themselves with communities sharing a rule of life, they are far from any formal authority structures.

One of the great encouragements of the research among Christians who are not engaged with a church congregation has been the variety and depth of Christian community and missional living that has been encountered.[44] Those who have applied the study of innovation to the Church are not surprised that it is where Christian life is practised on the edges of formal church organisations that new ways of expressing faith are encountered. New Zealand missiologist Steve Taylor, in his reflections on innovation in Christian history, identifies three conditions that seem to need to be present for ecclesiastical entrepreneurialism to prosper. Freedom from authority structures and regulation is vital, but so is the bringing together of different gifts, experiences and perspectives in a kind of 'cross-fertilisation'; so too is 'support', through financial provision, research and training.[45] Where attempts to catalyse innovation *within* church institutions have borne fruit, they try to provide these same conditions. At the time of the instigation of the fresh expressions movement and the Mission-Shaped Church report, Archbishop Rowan Williams spoke of the need for 'principled and careful loosening of structures'.[46] In practice this means more trust and less regulation, a deliberate relinquishing of control by giving people a free, or at least a loose, rein. In recent years pioneering movements have recognised the benefits of intentionally bringing together those of an entrepreneurial bent through 'incubators', where innovators can share their experiences with one another in an environment of mutual support.

---

44 Aisthorpe, *The Invisible Church*, pp. 167–84.

45 New Zealand missiologist Steve Taylor provides a helpful reflection on examples of innovation in Christian history and the characteristics of those situations that seem to catalyse and encourage a renewal of the Church: Taylor, S., 2019, *First Expressions: Innovation and the Mission of God*, London: SCM Press.

46 Croft, S., 'Fresh expressions in a mixed economy Church: a perspective', in Croft, S. (ed.), 2008, *Mission-Shaped Questions: Defining Issues for Today's Church*, London: Church House Publishing, p. 6.

Some landowners are allowing strips of land the freedom for rewilding, diverting some resources from what they see as their main crop, because they are recognising the wider benefits for the environment and sustainable production; those who control the resources of denominations need to be prepared to invest in ecclesial innovation without the expectation of payback for the institution, just for the health of the whole Church and its impact in the world.

From clericalism to everyone

In traditional denominations, control is often manifested as clericalism, where explicit policies about who can and cannot do various activities in the life of the Church are reserved for a small number of ordained professionals. These overt manifestations of clericalism are often endorsed and reinforced in more subtle ways, such as the ways in which congregational activities are choreographed. The word 'clericalism' is often associated with the Roman Catholic tradition, but is a phenomenon that is often at work wherever some of the gifts the Spirit gives the Church are valued more highly than others and where the giftedness of all people is not recognised and practised. It has become a focus of attention for the current Pope who observed in his *Letter to the People of God* in August 2018 that, 'Clericalism, whether fostered by priests themselves or by lay persons, leads to an excision in the ecclesial body that supports and helps to perpetuate many of the evils that we are condemning today.'[47] That word 'excision', usually used in a medical context, means 'the act of removing something' and what he was referring to was the elimination of 'the active participation of all the members of God's People'.

In some circles the term 'clericalism' has come to be associated with the scandal of horrific abuse in some parts of the

---

47 Pope Francis, 2018, 'Pope Francis: Letter to the People of God (full text)', 20 August, *Vatican News*, www.vaticannews.va/en/pope/news/2018-08/pope-francis-letter-people-of-god-sexual-abuse.html (accessed 17.01.2020).

Church. Indeed the Pope, in that same letter, stated emphatically that 'To say "no" to abuse is to say an emphatic "no" to all forms of clericalism.'[48] However, another tragedy of clericalism is the loss to the Church of the gifts and insights of people whose contributions are excluded by the dynamics of power – and the loss to those people of finding opportunities for the full expression of their faith. We tend to associate clericalism with 'high' church traditions, but the unhealthy elevating of some individuals or roles happens in all kinds of church congregations.

Remember Luke's account of the Twelve appointing the Seven in Acts chapter 6. The Apostles were confident that their God-given priority was a ministry of teaching the Word. However, a dispute related to food distribution was in danger of derailing the Christian fellowship in Jerusalem. Fuelled by underlying ethnic tensions, the situation was crucial and urgent. It demanded their attention. Surely, in the face of such a pressing and vital issue they could have set aside their own priorities, got things back on track – before returning to their own vocation. However, for the Twelve to intervene themselves would not only have taken them away from their own primary concerns, it would also have robbed others of their place in God's purposes. Unfortunately, many translations, in rendering the Apostles' words along the lines of 'It would not be right for us to neglect the ministry of the word of God in order to wait on tables'[49] suggest a differentiation in status between one task and another. In actual fact the word translated 'ministry' (*diakonein*) is applied to both tasks. Some are called to a 'ministry of the word'; others are called to a humanitarian ministry, which in this case was comprised of practical assistance to widows. *Both* tasks required servants 'full of the Spirit and wisdom'.[50]

In the New Testament the Greek verb to 'call' occurs about 150 times and there is no indication of a hierarchy of tasks. However, what Luke's account does imply is a direct link

48 Pope Francis, 'Letter to the People of God'.
49 Acts 6:2 (NIV).
50 Acts 6:3.

between the Twelve's courageous and prayerful delegation and what followed: 'So the word of God spread. The number of disciples in Jerusalem increased rapidly ...'[51] People thrive when they find opportunities to exercise their God-given talents and they wither when they find themselves squeezed into roles for which they are ill suited or burdened with responsibilities for which they have no sense of calling; all kinds of expressions of the Church flourish when they discard pre-existing blueprints and are shaped by the gifts of their members.

The 'bouncebackability' of the Church

In his recent book *On the Marsh*, sports journalist and naturalist Simon Barnes shares his experience of buying a small patch of marshland adjacent to his house. Barnes, writing with great love, describes his sensing the great value and potential in terms of habitat of this neglected wetland, his realising its vulnerability, and then his collaborating with others, but primarily with nature itself, in allowing its rewilding. Despite threats such as the chemical run-off from adjacent farmland creating a nettle monoculture, he chronicles the arrival of otters, six species of warblers, families of marsh harriers and dozens of other species of birds and mammals. Dipping into the vocabulary of football journalism, Barnes reflects on the 'bouncebackability' of nature. Like the volcanic wasteland of Mount St Helens, his modest corner of wetland demonstrates the resurrection power at work in the natural world.

Bouncebackability was not a word in the vocabulary of G. K. Chesterton, but it was the same phenomenon he described in his classic panorama of Christian faith in which he observes that, 'At least five times ... the Faith has to all appearance gone to the dogs. In each of these five cases it was the dog that died.'[52] The Church, with the power of the resurrected Jesus at its heart, has an unlimited capacity for bouncebackability.

---

51 Acts 6:7.

52 Chesterton, G. K. (first published 1925), 2014, *The Everlasting Man*, CreateSpace, p. 203.

Congregations die. Denominations die. Applying the words of Jesus, 'I will build my church, and the gates of Hades will not prevail against it'[53] in relation to any specific institutional expression of the Church is misplaced hope and delusional, but the Church, the body of Christ, will outlive all its challengers and challenges.

The attempted resuscitation of dying congregations is a tragic diversion and not to be confused with the resurrection of the Church. The former is often the preoccupation of the institutional centre; the latter tends to happen on the fringe. Attempts to resuscitate dying congregations usually involve adaptation, trying to find new answers to old questions, especially related to the how, what and when of congregational worship services in an effort to make them accessible and understandable to those who are not involved. The rewilding of the Church draws on the resurrection power at its heart through innovation, asking new questions and going back to foundational considerations, refocusing on following Jesus and loving neighbours and being open-minded about what emerges.

Let the rewilding begin

God is rewilding the Church. The wild Messiah cannot be tamed. That inexpressible power at the heart of the Church may be hindered by invasive species, but cannot be quenched. We too are summoned to *be* rewilded, urged to allow the Great Interferer to have his way, to transform us from the inside out. You and I are invited to cooperate with the great regeneration of creation and invited to be part of what is emerging. We are beckoned along that trajectory of hope, inspired and energised by the new-every-morning love of God. Hear the call to participate in the ultimate adventure. Jesus says, 'Follow me'.

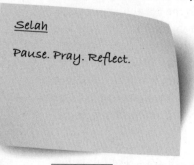

Selah

Pause. Pray. Reflect.

---

53 Matthew 16:18.

Index of Bible References

Index of Names and Subjects